Bull's Eyes

The selected memoirs of
Peter Bull

edited by Sheridan Morley,
with an introduction by
Robert Morley

Robin Clark Ltd
London

First published by Robin Clark Limited 1985
A member of the Namara Group
27/29 Goodge Street, London W1P 1FD

Copyright © 1985 Don Busby

British Library Cataloguing in Publication Data

Bull, Peter, 1912–1984
  Bull's Eyes: selected memoirs of Peter Bull.
  1. Bull, Peter, 1912–1984 2. Actors — Great
  Britain — Biography
  1. Title II. Morley, Sheridan
  792'.028'0924   PN2598.B74

ISBN 0-86072-095-0

Phototypeset by AKM Associates (UK) Ltd
Ajmal House, Hayes Road, Southall, Greater London
Printed and bound in Great Britain
by Nene Litho and Woolnough Bookbinding
both of Irthlingborough, Northants

For Mary Cook and Don Busby

Contents

Editor's Note

I am, I think, the eldest of Peter Bull's many godchildren and these memoirs, all about him and largely by him, are for the dozens of us who were his friends and the other thousands who were his readers, his stage and screen admirers, and sometimes also his customers and his collectors; for as well as being an author and an actor Peter was also, towards the end of his life, the proprietor of an astrological emporium and the greatest of experts on teddy bears.

He was also the man who taught me how to get around London on buses (suitably enough, since his brother was at the time in charge of London Transport) and where best to dive into the pool beneath the RAC Club in Pall Mall, quite apart from many other urban survival hints for a stagestruck teenager in the middle 1950s. He was a marvellous and kind and funny and touching and eccentric man, the most enchanting of godfathers and friends, and when he died at the age of seventy-two in May 1984 it seemed to me both strange and a little sad that many people instantly recalled him as the Bully Bear man but had forgotten some of the other aspects of a long and intriguing life. This anthology, which brings together a selection of his memoirs in one volume for the first time, is an attempt to recall the Best of Bull.

It is drawn from his magazine journalism and his six volumes of autobiography, all published between 1956 and 1973 but all out of print for more than a decade at the time of his death. A couple of those books were rightly hailed by Kenneth Tynan as being the funniest ever written by an actor, but only the first (*To Sea in a Sieve*) went into more than one edition, and towards the end of his life

Peter himself was among the collectors who could sometimes be found searching the shelves of secondhand bookshops in Chelsea for rare copies of *Bulls in the Meadows, I Know the Face but . . ., I Say, Look Here, It isn't All Greek to Me* and *Life is a Cucumber.*

Peter also published one comic novel (*Not on Your Telly!*) and four adult bear books (*Bear with Me, The Teddy Bear Book, A Hug of Teddy Bears* and *The Zodiac Bears*) as well as the *Bully Bear* adventures, a paperback series for children written at the end of his life. But I must confess I have largely avoided the bear material, partly because much of it is still available in the shops, as indeed are the Bully Bears themselves.

For permission to reprint articles and sections of text still in copyright other than that of the Bull estate, I am most grateful to the late Peter Davies, Robson Books, the editors and publishers of *Punch* and *World Medicine*, as well as to the House of Nisbet; while without the help and encouragement of Peter's friend and heir Don Busby, my search for much of his early magazine writing would have taken years. I would also like to thank Julian Bourne for his intelligence and perspicacity in bringing an initially massive manuscript down to publication size.

The arrangement of this book is essentially chronological, but a brief biographical note here might help to explain the various sections into which I have divided it. Peter was born on 21 March 1912, the youngest of the four sons of the Rt. Hon. Sir William Bull, for many years MP for Hammersmith. He was educated at Winchester and Tours University before starting a brief career as a journalist. By 1932 however he was studying acting with Elsie Fogerty, and in the following year made his first stage appearance at the Shaftesbury Theatre as the Janitor in *If I were You*. His next two years were spent in the West End and on Broadway playing small parts in *As You Desire Me* and *Escape Me Never* with Elisabeth Bergner.

In 1936 he returned to London to appear (again with Bergner) in *The Boy David* by J.M. Barrie. He then went into management, forming with my father and several others a repertory company at Perranporth in Cornwall. Productions there were interrupted by the war, which he fought with distinction in the Royal Navy, starting as an ordinary seaman and retiring in 1945 as a Lieutenant Commander with the DSC, an honour he only discovered he'd won when reading news of Old Boys in his school magazine.

Peter's war is recalled here in the third section of an anthology which elsewhere needs no footnotes or afterwords; but the writing of 'Anzio, Anzio, Anzio' (a chapter taken from *To Sea in a Sieve*) may well surprise readers accustomed to the lighter tone of Bully's postwar stage and screen reminiscences. His war was an often bloody and unpleasant one, made bearable only 'by Guess and by God' and by a remarkable, understated courage which took him from ordinary (or extraordinary) seaman to Lieutenant Commander. In this progress he was much aided by a loyal and beloved crew: 'Sandy' Horne, an ex-motor mechanic; Priest the signalman; Bill Knott, known as 'Knotty', and Trevor Goodwin the First Lieutenant, a quartet who first met Peter in the harbour at Greenock where he took command of the Landing Craft Flak that was so soon to see action off the Italian coast.

Returning to the theatre at the end of the war, Peter played Tappercoom in the first London and Broadway productions of Fry's *The Lady's Not for Burning*, Pozzo in the first London production of Beckett's *Waiting for Godot*, and Tetzel in the first London and Broadway productions of Osborne's *Luther*. His film career was no less distinguished, featuring appearances in *Oliver Twist*, *The African Queen*, *Tom Jones*, *Dr Strangelove*, *Dr Dolittle* and, a few months before his death, a brief but memorably weird farewell in drag as Queen Anne in *Yellowbeard*.

Through the 1950s, however, he became increasingly disenchanted with the life of an actor and discovered three other careers which gave him greater delight. First he wrote the autobiographies; then his fascination with the occult led him to open the Zodiac shop in Notting Hill Gate, selling all manner of things astrological; and finally he became recognized as one of the world's leading authorities on the history, care and psychology of the teddy bear. His own collection of two hundred bears was led by Aloysius, who achieved considerable fame by being carried by Sebastian Flyte through several episodes of *Brideshead Revisited*, and Bully Bear, who was the hero of many of his later books for children. His last book, published a few days after his death, was *The Zodiac Bears*, which neatly combined the three main interests of his later years: writing, astrology and bears.

Peter was unmarried, but leaves behind him a huge family of friends. One of the first and greatest of those is my father, whose memories of him go back half a century and who now writes the only other chapter of this anthology which is not by Bully himself.

Sheridan Morley

Introduction:
Perranporth and After
by Robert Morley

Peter Bull was a man who continuously wrote of his own memories and encounters with parents, friends and chance acquaintances, and he wrote in the manner of most occasional journalists: modestly depreciating himself, alive to his own follies and shortcomings, and leaving his reader just as the assailant was making the last punch and Peter having the last word. Like most of us, he may not actually have thought of that at the time, but left alone with the typewriter it made good reading.

His father, Sir William Bull, was a power not only in Hammersmith but also in the House of Commons. He wrote copiously in his own diaries of the progress of his four sons. Stephen, his eldest, was a social butterfly and, as when I first met him, was usually in white tie and tails awaiting a taxi-cab to take him to a rout. He was reported to be deeply in love with a daughter of the King of Spain and planned, so Peter told us, to marry her. With the coming of the war he was despatched to the Far East, became a prisoner of the Japanese and, force-marched on the way to construct a railway, suddenly sat down and died of exhaustion.

George, the second son, eventually succeeded to the Baronetcy and his father's practice as a solicitor. Anthony, the next brother, became, under Lord Ashfield, the controller of the London Underground system, and all three waited patiently for Peter to grow up.

His father occasionally shared their hopes and anxieties. He had been delighted, some years earlier, to herald Peter's entry into

Winchester by writing to his prep-school master congratulating him on achieving the apparently impossible feat of coaching his child through the Common Entrance, and confiding also his deep dislike of Peter's future housemaster. He then wrote to the latter, thanking him for accepting his child, and promptly put the letters in the wrong envelopes.

Peter made one or just possibly two friends at Winchester, but the housemaster was not either of them. Winchester taught him what most fat boys do well to learn early, the art of survival. Winchester and his mother taught him that. None of us who met her have ever quite forgotten Lady Bull who, widowed comparatively early in life, kept on the large house in Cadogan Gardens with Stephen perpetually dressing for dinner and an assorted bunch of actors and actresses rehearsing in the drawing room for the Perranporth summer theatre.

The idea of this commune first occurred to Peter on a visit to that hideous little Cornish town, and he rented the local hall on the spot and assembled a cast of his friends to amuse the natives and, during the peak season, the visitors. We were all to board with Bull and, at the end of the season, share with him in the box-office proceeds. Peter never actually told me that the holiday home he had rented for us was an old Cornish manor house with a creek at the bottom of the garden and an abundance of cedar trees, but that was somehow the impression I had formed. The shock therefore of finding that we were in fact billeted over a boot shop was speedily reinforced by the knowledge that our first task was to spend the first week not in rehearsal, but in packing away the resident's crockery and visiting various local well-wishers to ask if we could borrow their furniture in order to dress the stage. It was an ambitious and cunning notion which paid off well: for just as fond parents will attend school plays to catch a fleeting glimpse of their children, so patrons come eagerly to see their own armchairs or Welsh dressers displayed prominently on the set.

Once, when I had undertaken to direct one of our attractions, a member of the cast whom I had interrupted once too often while he was memorizing his lines set about all the props on stage and blitzed every stick of furniture with a chair leg.

But to return to Lady Bull, who understood her youngest child better than any of us. She was never anxious for him to grow up, which I suppose he never did, but she protected and cherished him and at times even praised us and provided tea after the rehearsals and apologized for the absence of jam in the sandwiches. 'My boys,' she used to say, 'are savoury boys.' Years later, when Peter invited her to (or was possibly unable to keep her away from) a matinée of *Waiting for Godot*, in which he created the part of Pozzo and charged around the stage secured by a noose to another actor pretending to be blind, Lady Bull was unabashed. She had brought her personal maid of many years, now her confidante, to the theatre, and when asked by Peter afterwards for a comment on the afternoon Lady Bull merely noted that Jessie had thought the orchestra-pit railing very well polished. It was her only comment: a generation protesting about Samuel Beckett.

But at Perranporth Peter chose all the plays and his mother would watch unconcerned from the stalls, sitting next to the mother of another of our little group, Frith Banbury, who was then also an actor. When either of their sons entered, the old ladies would lean forward suddenly with rapt attention: a pair of early talent spotters.

Considering that we never did anything even remotely *avant-garde*, and only seldom attempted a new play, the attention of the local press and even of the London critics was curiously sustained. Perranporth was a huge success until the war abruptly caused the little theatre to be closed, and almost immediately it was commandeered by a rival and equally dauntless impresario, Dame Marie Rambert.

Peter went to sea in command of a tank-landing craft and survived; but the horror of Dieppe and the beaches of Anzio, the blood and the death of his friends, he was to remember for the rest of his life. Ten years later he wrote of that naval war in his first book, *To Sea in a Sieve*, which Ludovic Kennedy called 'the very best type of naval war memoir'. Peter always chose the mask of comedy, but he kept the mask of tragedy in his bottom drawer and could not forget, even if he had wanted to do so.

Gossip, like gambling, either gets to you or it doesn't: Peter must have allowed several hours for it each morning. He was a living tape machine, forever reporting on the state of the human market with uncanny accuracy. Before the ink was dry on a contract he would be the first on the phone to congratulate; if a play was closing, he would be the first on the phone to alert you to the danger and to suggest a possible new avenue for exploration or employment. But to give the impression that he was a gossip-columnist without a column is misleading; his was a world of household names, at any rate in the acting profession, and they all without exception relied on him not to break their confidences, which he never did. Albert Finney, John Gielgud, Alec Guinness, Paul Scofield, Emlyn Williams, Harry Secombe, Elisabeth Bergner, Stewart Granger, Hermione Gingold, all were his confidants and all, where Peter was concerned, were inviolate. He seldom mixed his friends, and I am conscious that among the names I've mentioned are some who knew him better than I did. Perhaps we should have sought them out, jogged the memories, recorded the anecdotes; but that would have made a biography and this is essentially an autobiography.

Nor was I ever really competent to judge his acting, an art (or as I prefer to call it a trade) which he did not take very seriously. For most of the productions he appeared in he was the joker in the pack, a role to which his physical appearance made a considerable contribution. He was immensely stout, inheriting his father's physique as well as his fearlessness and originality of mind. Peter never got over what was to him the absurdity of being paid to enjoy himself. He did not so much court disaster as just happen to be on hand whenever a jester was needed, and sometimes when it wasn't. On the few occasions when he was provided with a role into which he could get his teeth, he was usually prevented from doing so because his bite was by that time impaired by an irresistible desire to giggle.

After Perranporth, his essays into theatrical management with my play *Goodness How Sad!* and Noel Langley's *Cage Me a Peacock* were financial disasters, and his relief when he finally persuaded himself to leave the stage was considerable. But if Peter was no longer to appear under the Big Top, he found a new profession among the sideshows. All his life he had been a showman, from the earliest days when, as a teenager in a hired dinner jacket, he sang or rather danced for his supper at the Embassy nightclub. He was paid for going there each evening with his lifelong partner Mary Cook and encouraging other dancers by taking to the floor as soon as the band struck up. They then had to stay dancing until at least seven other couples had followed their example; after that they were entitled to rest from their exertions and order scrambled eggs and bacon.

Much later in his life, Peter found a new career as an after-dinner, after-tea or after-lunch speaker; he joined the enormous cast of Associated Speakers and was kept running hither and thither from Felixstowe to Herne Bay in what was and still is the role of travelling storyteller or troubadour. 'Nowadays,' a prominent talks executive confided to me the other day, 'it is often, alas, a choice between affording the speaker or affording the soup, and you would be surprised how often the committees opt for the soup.' But in the halcyon days of the 1960s, Peter's programme was always fully booked.

I never knew exactly what form Peter's entertainment took, and I don't think his close friends were encouraged to attend, but he did once show me a sample programme when he was venturing into the American lecture market for the first time as a solo turn. 'They won't care for the recitations,' I told him, referring to the fairly lengthy excerpts he wished to interpolate from his own earlier performances as Buzfuz in *Pickwick* and the Bishop in *Luther*. 'I don't see why not,' he told me; 'besides, I had a terrible job learning them for the original productions, and one really must not waste material.' He was right, of course.

Peter had a horror, almost a mania, about extravagance of any sort; if he could get on a plane, a train, even a London omnibus paying less than the man who sat beside him, he was immensely heartened. On visits to America, he always travelled by charter and availed himself of every possible loophole open to the careful planner. Sometimes he crossed the Atlantic as a beekeeper, sometimes as a supporter of the Harrogate Baths Preservation Society, depending on who was offering the best rates for specialist group charters; often he would book himself on obscure airlines and route himself to New York via Rotterdam, Leipzig or Minneapolis. He never tired of pointing out that both ends of a Jumbo arrive at the same time and, having survived Winchester and the War, he was wonderfully able to ignore discomfort.

The only place where he lived extravagantly was Kentucky, where for some years he promoted the local Derby by way of a private radio station. 'One of my nice little contracts,' he told me afterwards, 'and of course I don't have to be there while the race is actually being run.'

Soon he had a host of friends in the USA and was constantly to be seen on television chat shows there. His hosts were enchanted by his impersonation of a fall guy who genuinely loved falling about. They kept tapes of his appearances and re-ran them constantly. How often, as one packed or unpacked a suitcase in an American hotel bedroom, and fiddled with the seventeen dials on the television set, did one come across Peter explaining how he cured himself of alopecia after wearing the rubber wig in *Godot*, or how he stole a scene in *Dr Dolittle* from a white rabbit, a vulture, a monkey, two parrots and a goat?

In the midst of all his other activities, Peter decided in the mid-1960s to open a shop. He had become increasingly interested in astrology, and by now any mention of a friend's behaviour or achievement was immediately associated with the star-sign under which he or she had been born. Considering the number of people obsessed by their horoscopes, the shop was a very good idea. I once asked him, though, if the struggle of running his Zodiac store, discreetly situated just behind Notting Hill Gate tube station, was really worth all the sweat it entailed – arriving at dawn to sweep out the premises, ordering and often marking down the stock, dealing with VAT inspectors and shoplifters and slow-paying customers and his one supreme patron, the Sultan of Oman. 'Yes,' said Bully, 'because I have now discovered that what I most enjoy in the world is giving change.'

Besides vast stocks of books, tumblers, handkerchieves, ashtrays, bookmarks and matchboxes all emblazoned with different star signs, Peter imported a genuine fortune-teller who attended the shop regularly to be consulted by the faithful. He took a percentage of her fees, and only stopped singing her praises when she failed to forewarn him of a break-in at the premises and a small fire in his King's Road flat. All seemed to go swimmingly for a while, but then Peter suddenly tired of the climb up the stairs to the coffee machine and the increasing violence of the local hooligans, so the shop was shut.

Only a few months before he died, he allowed his celebrated flat opposite the Chelsea Odeon to be inspected in his absence by a breakfast-television detective who was supposed to deduce from its contents the occupation, purpose, ambitions and maybe even identity of the owner. The detective was obviously deeply confused by what he found there, and came up with the solution that the flat was being shared by two extremely strange individuals. Puzzled by the plethora of teddy bears, and alarmed by one clad entirely in black leather, he opined that one or possibly both the occupants were, if not criminally insane, at least capable of extreme violence. When Peter turned for consolation to his oldest and closest friend, Mary Cook, she offered no sympathy. 'The trouble with you,' she said not entirely unperspicaciously, 'is that you have always been mad for publicity.'

Now it may or may not have been true that, at the time of the breakfast-television man's visit, the flat was also being used by someone whom I might euphemistically refer to as a gentleman lodger. The boyish and (to an old square such as myself) absurd homosexual infatuations of my old friend were something we never discussed, and they played no part at all in our friendship.

There is a line in one of Lonsdale's plays to the effect that when you enter someone's life as a friend, go in instantaneously, and when you leave it, go even more quickly. Once you were a friend of Peter's, he never let you out of his life. He had always kept his friends, except in those terrible war years, and he was determined never to lose any more.

When the day came for his funeral, Chelsea Old Church was

crammed but, save for my fellow actors, I hardly knew anyone; Peter never mixed his friends. Yet he was the most expert friend I ever had. He knew our birthdays, our children's birthdays, our wedding anniversaries. He wrote to us constantly, visited us when we were in ill health, and on every possible occasion sent a postcard with a view of Sidmouth or a portrait of José Collins in *Maid of the Mountains* or an unknown bullfighter to mark whatever the occasion was.

In the late 1960s, returning from a lecture tour in the United States, Peter decided to write the first of his many books on teddy bears. He announced in *The Times* that he was preparing a symposium, and invited the bears themselves or their owners to contribute. When Peter was about sixteen his mother had given his own bear to the dustmen and he sustained a sense of permanent loss for the rest of his life, or so he maintained. His world from now on was peopled by every species of little (or quite large) furry monsters, as well as their owners, some of whom had been similarly traumatized in childhood by the loss of their bears; others managed still to cling on to them.

When his *Bear with Me* first appeared in 1969, Peter's financial future was assured. Publishers, toymakers and promoters of carnivals suddenly discovered that there was a fortune in bears, and Peter was in constant demand for every kind of teddy-bear picnic. He had a bear named after him, and wrote a series of children's books linking his Bully Bear with celebrated department stores, stately homes and most particularly America, where he correctly estimated there was a large and comparatively untapped bonanza. There were some of his friends who, like myself, looked askance. Either you're into bears or you're not.

In the end, I suppose the bears killed him. He was no longer in good health, and his schedule was far too strenuous. He ignored medical advice to slow down, refused to pay sufficient attention to diabetes, declined to listen to the murmurs of his own heart and bought, a week before he died, a Will form at Boots and because of the determinedly joky way in which he filled it in, very nearly managed to die intestate. Luckily there was an earlier document drawn up by his solicitor brother, and between the two wills some sort of order was maintained.

Blissfully unaware of the legal confusion he was about to cause, Peter suffered a fatal heart attack and, after a few days in intensive care, left the stage. What made his loss so deeply felt by all his friends was the knowledge that we were never again to know anyone remotely like him. His genius was not for acting, or writing, or lecturing, or being the greatest expert on teddy bears. His genius was for making friends and keeping them. I was lucky enough to be one of them.

Robert Morley

PART ONE

You Ought to Go off the Stage

1
Escape Me Never

I had better confess at the outset that I am an actor. I am telling you this now so that those allergic to theatrical biographies may be spared a return trip to their lending libraries. Not that this is the usual story of 'Seven Steps to Stardom' or 'Discovered Genius in the West Cromwell Road'. It is simply the tale of a busker who is at the crossroads.

For a quarter of a century I have been connected with the theatre, and until very recently was certain that I had no intention of severing the ties which bound me to it. A few years ago, however, I had the good fortune to stumble on a sideline, and thanks to indulgent publishers and you, dear readers, I have been encouraged to pursue this new profession with enthusiasm and indeed financial reward. It is a quieter and less nerve-racking way of making a living, and it is impossible to ignore a whisper that echoes through my brain to the tune of 'You ought to go off the stage. You ought to go off the stage.'

In my frequent fantasies concerning my obituary I see a simple tombstone or urn with the following inscription on it:

HERE LIES PETER BULL
WHO MISSED THE BUS
WITHOUT MAKING ANY SERIOUS ATTEMPT
TO CATCH IT.

And it would be a true epitaph, causing me to reflect that perhaps I have wasted my entire life. Yet I cannot consider myself a tragic figure, having loved the theatrical profession for so long; and this book is to explain to you (and incidentally myself) why I feel any drastic decision must be the outcome of a complete stocktaking. My other aims are: (a) to try to discourage those with a tiny talent, or no talent at all, from joining an overcrowded profession, and (b) to make enough money to get a step nearer to leaving the stage.

I doubt if I shall succeed in either of these, but while we are waiting to see the outcome, I had better get on with the saga which has put me in such a quandary. But how to begin? I must study other theatrical biographies and see how they cope with this problem.

Yes, I see. I have to trace any hereditary talent. That's easy. No one ever used the magic phrase 'You ought to go on the stage' to me, but my Aunt Norah (on my mother's side) was on tour with *The Private Secretary* at the turn of the century, and later understudied in something called *Leah Kleschna* at Drury Lane Theatre, before retiring from the stage at the age of thirty. Her stage name was Nora Gray, a pseudonym which she also adopted for her literary career, during which she wrote very romantic short stories for a publication entitled *The Blue Magazine*, which was not the sort of journal you might think. It is, however, fair to assume that she passed on both her gifts to me.

Other theatrical connections were my Uncle Jocelyn (a tiny uncle, also on my mother's side) who had written several successful plays, had an enormous moustache and liked to feed the pigeons in Trafalgar Square, and a Mme Sarah Bernhardt, whose business affairs were administered by my solicitor grandfather (on my mother's side).

I have not as yet mentioned my father's side, but everyone was on it when he refused point-blank to let me tread what are laughingly known as 'The Boards'. My desire to plunge into the theatrical world attacked me very early on in life, and even at school I was kept busy writing to actresses for their photographs. These I stuck up in my study until my housemaster ordered me to tear them down. It was 1927 and pride of place went to June, José Collins and, of course, Miss Tallulah Bankhead. My mentor said he would not have the place defiled by actresses, so I stuck up a picture of Mr Paul Robeson which cost me six strokes on the b.t.m. But all this sort of thing made me feel very sophisticated and hardly able to bear my housemaster's lecture on sex to those leaving, which practically began:

'You may have noticed between your legs . . .'

In the holidays I was seldom out of the theatre, and read everything I could lay my hands on about the subject. Yet I knew I did not necessarily want to be an actor. I just desired vaguely to be connected with 'the stage'. To be someone's secretary or dresser was the sort of appointment I had in view, but my parents did not seem all that keen on the idea. I was packed off post-haste to the University of Tours, where I had an ecstatic five months. The trouble was that I never met any French people and my letters home seem to have created a bad impression. After a vivid account of a fancy-dress dance in which I unwisely described the costumes in which my partner and I were arrayed, my father arrived out of the blue and whisked me back to London where I would have more limited opportunities of appearing as a tomato, accompanied by a young lady in a top hat and virtually nothing else.

My father wanted me to be a chartered accountant, a profession which seemed to me to lack glamour. However, in order to show willing, I did settle for 'journalism'. Through influence I joined an organization known in those days as 'The Great Eight', consisting as it did of that number of illustrated journals, headed by the *Tatler* and the *Illustrated London News*. In theory I was to work my way through all the departments and I started by canvassing for advertisements for the *Tatler*, graduating to the editorial columns of this paper, and for an all too brief moment my brother and I were 'Eve' of 'The Letters of Eve' while someone was on holiday. My bro. was a sort of Débutante's Delight and as such was invited EVERYWHERE, and thus could give me all the more lurid details of Society which supplemented my contribution. I went to first nights in the gallery with my mother's binoculars, and gave totally incorrect descriptions of What They Were Wearing. Between us, we used to pep up the columns quite a tidge, until a couple of threatened libel actions stopped us being 'Eve' and I went back to counting the number of words in the articles.

Later I was transferred to the *Graphic*, which was unfortunately very much on the skids at the time, and shortly after my arrival turned into something called the *National Graphic*, printed on rather common paper, and sold at sixpence a week instead of a shilling. My salary – four pounds a week – happily remained the same, but not for long. The paper passed into oblivion and I left the building. Before I did this, however, I noticed in the lift a tall, slender young man going up to the top floor to do a bit of drawing. He turned out afterwards to be Michael Wilding, but as he didn't notice me, the whole of this paragraph is a waste of time, except that I was told by the publishers I must bring in a few names fairly early on. All theatrical biographies do.

I then went to Odhams Press, where I joined a paper called the *Ideal Home*, for which I was an advertising representative. I hated this job, because it meant my trying to persuade firms into taking space by convincing them that it was worth a vast expenditure. To complicate matters, I had to bring in a certain amount of money every month, which resulted in my going round to my friends about the twenty-ninth of each month and browbeating them into action. My principal friend was an enchanting lady called, then, Susan Tilney, who owned a firm called 'Susan's Inventions' which constructed a large number of the most bizarre labour-saving devices that I have clapped my peepers on. One was 'The Eiderdowner', which consisted of two clips to keep the eiderdown from slipping off the bed. Then there was the 'Dirty Dog Bag' for keeping your dog in if it was wet and muddy, and your own dogs in if they were ditto, if you follow me. A cushion that you strapped on to yourself for use in trains was another ingenious idea, and a 'Garden Horse' for sitting on when reading had many devotees, including the late Queen Mary. It was also equipped with numerous sockets and pockets for keeping tools, seeds and hoses in. I remember also a rather snobby stick for attaching money to when one was out hunting and some kind agricultural minion opened the gate to you. Susan Tilney used to travel a great deal by train surrounded by and/or wearing all her inventions, which caused a good measure of curiosity and resultant business. There is no record, however, of her sitting in the corridor astride the 'Garden Horse'.

But in spite of her generosity and that of other friends in the world of commerce, I was unable to make good, and was sacked from the *Ideal Home*, and this disaster coincided with the death of my father. What to do? I inserted an advertisement in *The Times*, drawing attention to my qualifications, and asking for suggestions. This resulted in one letter from a nudist camp which I didn't follow up. I was by now twenty-one years of age, and, in my opinion, pretty promising material for something. I had an idea that my mother did not mind quite so much about my stage interests as my father had done, and I determined to go ahead. I decided that I must have something called 'training', so for a few weeks I had splendid private voice-production lessons from Miss Elsie Fogerty, the doyenne of The Central School of Dramatic Art, which operated in the Royal Albert Hall in those days. The lessons consisted mainly of feeling Miss Fogerty's stomach when she was speaking and her feeling my stomach when I was speaking. It sounds sexy but wasn't. I then bought a copy of her book called *Speechcraft* which I didn't quite understand, and asked her for a bill, which she never gave me. She was a great lady, and it is perhaps fortunate that she did not live long enough actually to catch me at it.

I was by now fully equipped to embark on my stage career, or so I imagined. Not for me the hard way with a talent like mine; no repertory theatres, no fit-up tours, whatever they are, or one-night stands. I was to give myself to London in my full glory, and wrote off to every manager whose address I could find. My best bet was Charles B. Cochran, who had been a client of Bull and Bull and a close friend of my father, and he very kindly got his production manager, the late Frank Collins, to give me the once-over. Mr Collins quite rightly suggested that I should get a bit of experience before playing a leading part in a Cochran production, so I graciously said I would.

To my amazement Sydney Carroll, to whom I had also written, sent for me and, after introducing me to his director, Maxwell Wray, gave me thirty shillings a week and at least two non-speaking parts in a play called *If I were You*. The piece, which was about Jewish pogroms in Russia, opened on 15 June, 1933, and ran for every one of eight performances at the now defunct Shaftesbury Theatre. Owing to the number of tickets I dished out for the first night, I was a good deal out of pocket by the end of the run. I played a noisy Russian student in the first act swinging an empty champagne bottle round my head, and a very old janitor in the last act. As I have always gone the whole hog with character make-up, without any knowledge to back the hog up, my make-up bills were stupendous. I was, of course, completely recognizable in both roles.

Also in the cast were Augustus Yorke, the original Potash or Perlmutter in the play of those names, and a wonderful old character actress called Joan Pereira, who was to have a big effect on my career. Playing a student in the first act and a policeman in the third was the now famous director, Frith Banbury. He spent a lot of money on make-up too, but had been fully trained, or so he said, and impressed me enormously. We became great friends, and every single night each of us took one arm of Joan Pereira across the road in order to catch her bus. There were only six buses in actual fact, because she did not go home after the two matinées. The first night was attended by a large proportion of my family and friends, none of whom were committal about the play or my chances of achieving stardom overnight. The last night was attended, as far as I can remember, by no one at all.

Frith and I were out of work as a result, but we had no intention of 'resting', and we decided to get into some Sunday shows while awaiting our next assortment of roles. In those days there were a great many societies banging away on Sunday nights, and they were not taken as seriously as they are now. A few reputable ones like the Repertory Players were in existence, but they were highly professional and not a suitable playground for beginners. We did manage, however, to get into a lovely play called *Dath* which was put on by The 1930 Players in 1933 for two pretty astonishing performances at the Ambassadors Theatre. It was about ancient Britain, and was written by Miss Bertha Graham, the chairlady of The 1930 Players. Frith played a captain of the army and I was most of the army for most of the rehearsals. Indeed, I can well remember him saying: 'Are you with me, men?' to which I replied, 'Yes.' I think it was my best line.

Also in the cast were Catherine Lacey, Leo Genn, Harold Clayton, and a loaf of bread which, for reasons best known to itself, rolled about the stage a great deal during the Monday matinée and caused vast merriment both sides of the footlights. By Monday the news had spread round the theatrical profession like a forest fire and the theatre was crammed from top to bottom with earnest students of contemporary drama. Miss Graham had brought in a lot of her friends to play captive lady Britons, and I had to bind them up a good deal, which was very difficult as they struggled like maniacs, not having attended many rehearsals. I remember many notable lines in the play, and it is difficult to forget a character called Eine, the Herb Woman, played with élan by Miss Inez Bensusan, who at the dress-rehearsal had forgotten a fairly essential 'prop', and announced on the stage, 'I am Eine, the Herb-Woman.' There was then a long pause before she hissed into the wings, 'I've forgotten the herbs,' which were thrown on by the distraught stage-manager, and the set suddenly resembled Culpepper House. Other lines that stick in one's memory are, 'Brazen, the Tall, bring up the rear'; and 'Agg, let us go fishing in the lower pool.' The latter line was assigned to Mr Banbury, who for obvious reasons found it rather difficult to deliver at the second performance. The entrance of the captive lady Britons was heralded by, 'Who are these in gorgeous raiment?' which was a slight case of the misapplied adjective. For Miss Graham had ransacked her attic and/or bottom drawers for the company, and everything from deer's antlers to Victorian button boots was being handsomely displayed.

After this extravagant exercise, Frith and I went from strength to strength and got splendidly involved in an organization known as The Tempest Theatre which was run by two young gentlemen, one of Swedish extraction, who took themselves v. seriously indeed. Readings took place on the third floor of a house in Percy Street to the accompaniment of a strong smell of frankincense and myrrh and some rather hairy nuts which were offered between the acts. They organized entertainments for Sunday nights at the Fortune Theatre, and the first one in which I appeared was called *Perdican and Camilla* about which I can remember very little, but the play was preceded by an unforgettable lady called Valeska Gert who mimed everything including, I regret to say, 'Being A Baby'. This consisted largely of blowing bubbles out of her mouth, which plunged the audience into ecstasy and caused her to run off shouting 'Ich habe nimmer getanzt für eine solche Publik' or some such phrase. However, she did say to Mr Banbury, 'Ich finde das Bull ist gut als komiker,' which Frith still puts in some of his first-night telegrams to me.

The Tempest Theatre's next contribution to the history of the drama was a German play called *Leonce and Lena*, which provided me with the part of either King Pipi of Popo or King Popo of Pipi. It was a very big part and I was given dressing room No 1 at the Fortune Theatre, but I was not helped in my rendering of the role by Mr Banbury who was playing the subsidiary part of The Chancellor and kept on saying, 'Tut, tut, your Majesty,' whether it was in the script or not. The producer, Herr Mellinger, had been rather sharp during rehearsals, and had once said to Mr Banbury, 'You must not make nonsense with yourself, Mr Banbury,' whatever that could possibly mean. The dress-rehearsal was a notable one, as he had engaged a lot of art school students to what's known as 'walk-on' in the production. He was not entirely prepared to find that these artistes had walked off and were indulging in what can only be described as sexual intercourse underneath the stage. This gave a slightly ragged touch to the dress-rehearsal, during which Mrs Louis Kentner (a darling and lovely lady then called Griselda Gould) fell through a soap box not once but twice. She had also to do a good deal of running in order to avoid being pinched by at least two of the character actors and those of the art school who were not otherwise employed. The behaviour of Miss Gould, Mr Banbury and myself throughout this production unfortunately prevented us from being asked to appear in any other Tempest Theatre project, and one of the directors married Miss Valeska Gert.

Mr Banbury and I then had to part company, and he went into a series of commercial productions. I, on the other hand, joined the extreme *avant-garde* theatre of this time, viz. the Gate Theatre Studio in Villiers Street, a tiny building of enormous reputation and minute salaries. The sanitary arrangements for the artistes were plain and simple, as buckets were cheerfully provided in each of the dressing-rooms (two). I obtained this job entirely through the efforts of Miss Joan Pereira who rang me up and ordered me to report to Mr Peter Godfrey, who was at that time running the theatre. She was pretty cryptic on the blower, and instructed me to say 'Yes' when Mr Godfrey asked me if I spoke German. As the only German I knew had been picked up from Valeska Gert or Mr. Banbury imitating Valeska Gert, I could not help thinking that I was courting disaster, but off I tootled to be given a script of *As You Desire Me* by Pirandello. I was to study the part of the doctor in the last act and to come back after lunch and read it to Mr Godfrey. Mystified and alarmed by the discovery that the entire role was in German, I stood about wondering what to do for the best when Miss Pereira emerged from the lady's loo (for the use of the audience usually), and told me to meet her in the ABC up the street in ten mins. I carried out her instructions, and Joan taught me the part parrot-fashion over 'poached eggs on toast twice'. I went back, read it to the bearded Mr Godfrey, accepted the one pound a week offered as salary, and decided that I was an actor at last.

The cast was a highly distinguished one in the light of what has since occurred. It was headed by one of the most exciting personalities I have ever known, Jean Forbes-Robertson, who moved me so much in the play that I used to find myself trying to stop the tears coming to my eyes on the stage, which would not quite have fitted in with the character of the phlegmatic German doctor I was meant to portray. Also in the cast were Alastair Sim, Glen Byam-Shaw and Alan Webb. The maximum salary at the theatre was three pounds a week. I kept mousy quiet about my lack of German until one night I was summoned by Miss Forbes-R, who was not a one to mince matters.'

'You don't understand a word of German, do you, Peter?' she asked bluntly. I saw my pound a week vanishing in front of my eyes, but she had called me Peter.

'No,' I admitted. Miss Forbes-R roared with laughter, and that was all that happened until the next evening's performance. I came on to the stage to deliver my opening line which was 'Hat sie eine rote Nabe auf ihre Brüste?' which means (or so Joan Pereira assured me), 'Has she a red mark on her bust?' I delivered the line as best I could under the circumstances. The circumstances included Miss F.R. and Messrs Webb and Byam Shaw trembling on the brink of hysterical laughter. I got through the rest of my lines in a high falsetto and made a not very graceful exit. It was my first contact with the appalling malady which affects most actors, and which is almost impossible to explain to laymen. Something which does not seem remotely funny to the onlooker or even in retrospect, can plunge whole casts into hysteria, and a scene, or indeed a whole play, may be wrecked by a tiny untoward slip of the tongue or the behaviour of a hitherto inanimate object.

As a result, I came to dread doing the scene and was bitterly ashamed of myself. One night, after a deplorable exhibition, the Messrs Webb, B-S and I stayed behind, just saying the lines over and over again, laughing like maniacs until we were tired and bored. Needless to say, next night, I was off like a soda-water siphon once more.

As You Desire Me was a great success, and we ran six weeks to packed houses, and during the run I was summoned by the great Charles Cochran himself, who said that his Mr Collins had seen me in the piece (it must have been one of my comparatively normal nights) and had reported favourably. He was prepared, he said, to offer me a minute part or parts and/or an understudy in one of his two forthcoming productions. The choice was between an adaptation of Louis Golding's *Magnolia Street* which was to be done in a very spectacular way by Komisarjevsky, or a play starring Elisabeth Bergner, who was about to make her début in England in Margaret Kennedy's *Escape Me Never*, adapted from her book *The Fool of the Family*. Komisarjevsky was also to direct this, and as I had just seen Bergner in a film called *Der Traumende Mund*, and thought her nothing short of miraculous, the choice was an easy one. In actual fact *Magnolia Street* ran only six weeks, and *Escape Me Never* was to keep me fully employed for about two years.

I was to be paid four pounds ten shillings per week and the only part specified in my contract was that of a waiter. Flushed with excitement, before rehearsals I started taking lessons both in French and German from my friend Joan Pereira, who was about vingty-lingual, in her flat in the Vauxhall Bridge Road. I was not allowed to speak anything but German or French from the moment she opened the door, and our conversation was in consequence pretty peculiar. Miss Pereira would say 'Ich habe die Molly Hamley-Clifford in das Arts Theatre Club gesehen,' which meant that she had met another character actress called Molly Hamley-Clifford in the Arts Theatre Club. (Or perhaps you'd guessed that?) But all this training was to come in extremely useful when I played parts like the German Captain in *The African Queen* in full German (subsequently dubbed by Walter Rilla).

Rehearsals for *Escape Me Never* started in October 1933 and were vastly exciting. The first one was held at His Majesty's Theatre and the cast seemed enormous. There were some distinguished names to bandy around, like Leon Quartermaine, Hugh Sinclair, dear old Katie Johnson, and the splendid Edgar Wallace actor called Cronin Wilson.

Miss Bergner had us all at her feet from the moment she passed through the swing doors, tiny in an enormous fur coat. It wasn't until later that she also brought her huge sheepdog who was called Boompsie. She was to revolutionize my ideas about acting, as most of her effects were made either with her back to the audience or standing stock still with the minimum of gesture. We were to open at the Opera House, Manchester, and before we arrived there the whole undertaking was underplayed and there was very little advance publicity. But the first-night audience in Manchester cheered the place down, and Miss Bergner took about twenty solo calls. The next day the papers were ringing her praises, and it was quite obvious that we were in for a great success. She was in those early days quite petrified with nerves and misery, and I, in the role of a very old porter, with beard and fairly full character make-up, had to carry her on for her first entrance. I sometimes had to pursue her from the far corner of the stage, or even her dressing-room.

The first night in London was one of those legendary affairs that really happened. We opened at the Apollo Theatre on 8 December 1933, and it was very difficult to get the audience to leave the theatre. I remember Elisabeth B in the coffee stall scene saying under her breath, 'They don't like it, they don't like it,' but within a few minutes it was patent that she had made one of the biggest successes in theatrical history. It was to be an hilarious, happy and sensational run. I was kept busy changing from being an old porter into a young waiter, and then a singing customer at a coffee stall. As usual, all three roles were clearly recognizable from the front. I had a line or two as the waiter, and one got 'a Laugh'. My whole existence in those days hinged on the public's reaction to the laugh line, which I tabulated in my diary every night, giving myself marks out of a hundred. The scene took place on an old hotel terrace in the Dolomites and two middle-aged English spinsters were fumbling in their phrase-books. Finally, 'Due caffé neri,' they said to the plumpish waiter. The plumpish waiter replied, 'Two black coffees, yes, madam' in faultless English. Money for old rope.

This was the part of the play I liked best. After Miss Bergner had settled down and relaxed a bit, she gave the old porter in the first act some pretty tough handling, particularly at matinées. She used to tear his beard and moustache off, and throw them on the floor, leaving him facing upstage naked and giggling. I got my own back in the second act by bringing her and Hugh Sinclair a bill, on which I used to write tiny obscenities in the hope of making them laugh. They remained frozen faced at my efforts until I went a hundred and forty-five times too far by writing on the bill one matinée: 'Two lumps of bull – price 2s. 6d.' Miss Bergner, in a crystal-clear voice which rang through the old-ladies-filled audience, said: 'What does bull mean, Sebastian?', knowing perfectly well the answer. Bedlam ensued, and I got the sack from the rightly livid stage-director. Miss Bergner intervened and I was reinstated, and for at least two perfs wrote quite ordinary things on the bill, which made me even more hysterical.

The run was nothing if not eventful, and at the end of three months an astonishing thing happened. Elizabeth was taken suddenly ill during the first act and when she should have made her entrance, the curtain was lowered. Her understudy was a charming and talented girl called Betty Lynne, who had won the Gold Medal at the Royal Academy of Dramatic Art. She had made a small success as the pathetic chambermaid in *Grand Hotel*, and from what I had seen at understudy rehearsals was more than capable of giving an exciting performance. But on this occasion, 'The Theatre' was at its cruellest. The management decided to suspend the run until Miss Bergner's recovery, the curtain was rung down, Hugh Sinclair had to make a speech explaining the illness of our star, money was returned to the audience, and Miss Lynne's theatrical heart was broken. Shortly afterwards she left the stage.

But for the rest of the cast, the suspension was a fortunate one. We were all put on half-pay, and I went off on a holiday to Cornwall, and ended up at a small seaside resort called Perranporth. This event was to reshape my whole life, because two years later, with Robert Morley, Roger and Judith Furse, Frith Banbury and others, I was to run a summer theatre in the Women's Institute, which was to provide us all with some fairly remarkable experiences. It is another story, and frankly another book (memo for my dear publishers), but as a 'trailer' I would like to provide one or two extraordinary facts about the enterprise.

The stage at the beginning of our tenancy measured just six and a half feet by twelve, which slightly restricted movement. This handicap was increased by the fact that there was only one proper exit, apart from the back door of the actual building, which came in the middle of the stage and led straight into the backyard. This meant that on wet nights we had to provide a 'duty watch' of umbrella-carriers for those using this mode of exit.

Except for a carpenter there were no salaried personnel, and there was a general dish-out of profits at the end of the season. As the hall held only two hundred seats, the margin was narrow. But I took a house for the season, and provided board, lodging, hairdressing, haircuts, Cornish cream and indeed the highest teas ever served in the Western Hemisphere. The whole thing worked out pretty miraculously owing to the talents and dispositions of those with whom I was associated. It was, I think, the only repertory theatre in

England to have occasional hampers from Fortnum and Masons, and certainly the only one where the larger members of the cast (no names, no pack drill) had to go round testing the deck-chairs before each performance. This involved having to PRETEND to be rolling out of one's seat with laughter in order to give it a proper rehearsal.

The work involved was tremendous, because at one time we were doing four plays a week, but later in the season we kept on repeating the programme to fit in with the influx of fresh visitors. We did three brand-new plays, one of which, *Goodness, How Sad!* was written for the company by Robert Morley and played in London subsequently, for eight months. But that also is another story, and I must go back to the Apollo Theatre to resume my three roles in *Escape Me Never*.

We had had a four weeks' lay-off, and the next startling event of the run was the tragedy of Cronin Wilson. He was plainly very ill indeed, but insisted on continuing until one night he found himself on the stage fighting for breath and unable to utter. It was a scene with Hugh Sinclair, who gave on this occasion the most remarkable virtuoso performance that I can remember. He managed to twist his own lines so that the plot was sustained, and the audience actually noticed nothing wrong. But poor Cronin Wilson had played his last scene, and died in his dressing-room later that night. Tristram Rawson took over, and continued to play until the autumn. There was never even an empty box, and we were naturally flabbergasted when the notice suddenly went up. Apparently Miss Bergner was tired and was committed to a film in the near future. She had, however, promised Cochran that she would appear in New York in the play the following year, and that was that.

We were all deeply upset and, I regret to say, felt hard done by. But in conclave with some other members of the company, a pretty peculiar plan for our reimbursement was devised. We bought up every ticket we could lay our hands on for the last night from the box-office and the agents, advertised our wares in *The Times*, and took a furnished flat in Old Burlington Gardens to carry out our nefarious business. We engaged a sinister messenger to open and close the door, take the actual cash and run out in the streets to bring us double brandies. At first the demand was splendid, and we even got as much as ten pounds for a thirteen-and-sixpence stall, but suddenly the bottom dropped out of the market and we found ourselves faced with a lot of empty seats on our hands. The last day of all, to cut our losses, we sold some of them at cost price, and raced to the theatre in order to play our roles for what amounted to a highly personal audience.

It was actually a sad evening for all of us, and I seem to recall bursting into tears at one period of the evening, feeling that I would never have a happier and more glamorous engagement again. I didn't know that it was nowhere near the end of *Escape Me Never* as far as I was concerned.

For the next few months, I set about getting all the work I could find. I made my film début in something called *The Secret Voice*, which was so secret that it only made the Broadway Gardens Cinema in Walham Green one Sunday night. I got involved in a fairly off-beat theatre in South Kensington, which was started by a lot of Chelsea residents, including the entire Furse family, Anthony Quayle, Andrew Cruickshank, Reginald Beckwith, Nicholas Phipps, among others. Perfs took place in the Imperial Institute Cinema, and one had to pass a lot of curious exhibits on the way to one's seat. They did *Anna Christie* and *Liebelei*, and I wedged myself into a faintly improper play called *I was Waiting for You* which didn't actually set South Ken. on fire. But there were some very funny and delightful people connected with the venture, which made it a happy engagement.

The next improbable set-up with which I got connected was the Left Theatre, who produced plays which were Communist propaganda of the most violent sort. I enjoyed them hugely. We played the Phoenix Theatre for two Sundays in succession, and then did the rounds of the town halls, ranging from Stepney to Battersea. I carried a copy of the *Tatler* with me everywhere to avoid misunderstanding, and played Capitalist Pigs who always got their comeuppance before the end of the evening. The financial reward was slightly above the normal Sunday play 'expenses', and it was comforting to have people come up after the performance saying they had got the Message. The plays were produced by a splendid lady dictator called Barbara

Nixon, and were meaty stuff crammed with court scenes, prison scenes and a great many parts. The two productions with which I was associated were *Peace on Earth* and *Mother*.

At the risk of involving all those concerned, including myself, with the UnBritish Activities Tribunal, I would like to draw your attention to the programme of Gorki's *Mother*. I find that I played 'Court Official', 'Village Police Officer' and 'Prosecuting Attorney'. I remember the last role best, because it was when beating the hell out of it at either the Islington or East Ham Town Hall that I fell through several soap boxes with a clatter that collapsed the cast, and some of the floor of the Islington or East Ham Town Hall, and, I believe, converted a great number of political waverers. The action of Act One took place in 'The Mother's Cottage', 'A Cemetery' and 'Outside The Factory Gates', which will probably give you some idea of the plot. I do remember certain members of the cast, like Mark Dignam, André Van Gyseghem and Tony Beckwith, but I can't actually put faces to Dorrit Pemberton, Winnie Osgood, A. Goldstein, R. Katz, J. Yason, or indeed, I'm sorry to say, S. Yason. But of course Ben Vynreb was the assistant stage manager, and it says in the acknowledgements, 'Red Flag kindly lent by the Group Theatre', which was very civil of them.

After these capers, *Escape Me Never* popped up again, to my huge delight. First, I was asked to play one of my original parts (The Gent At The Coffee Stall) in the film, but alas and alack, like so many of my contributions to the Bioscope, I was left making faces on the cutting-room floor. But later in the year (1935), I was summoned to the Cochran office and asked to go to New York in the play. I was amazed and once more at Miss Bergner's tiny feet, as apparently she had refused to go unless the entire company went with her. I was to get fifty dollars a week, which in those days was quite adequate as a living wage. We played a limited season at the Shubert Theatre, and Elisabeth repeated her triumph. I was engaged as her personal bodyguard, in order to escort her through the wild fans who congregated outside the stage door.

I was fascinated by New York, terrified by the pace and noise, and lived first at a not very old-fashioned hotel, where they lodged you for a fixed price and threw breakfast in. And when I say 'threw breakfast in', I mean threw breakfast in. It was done through a slot in the door, and was enclosed in a large cardboard box. A friend of mine found a mouse in his, and when he politely said he would prefer not to have a mouse with his breakfast, they asked him to leave. Later, I moved to a strange apartment where I slept in a cupboard, and was relieved and delighted when the run came to an end, and I could return to quiet, dreary London.

I came back with only four ambitions in mind: to learn a little about acting (if poss.), to go to Hollywood, to have my own theatre, and not to be a star. All these I achieved in three years, with varying results.

2
Two Ambitions Quenched in Two Years

After my visit to New York, my immediate aim was to secure employment in a Repertory Theatre, where I hoped to bamboozle them a bit with my American reputation. But it was not easy, and there were the usual stumbling-blocks of entire companies already engaged for entire seasons, etc. After a series of abortive attempts I managed to wangle a Special Week at the Opera House, Coventry, in *Clive of India*. The casting for 'extra parts' was done from a strange little office in St Martin's Lane run by a witty lady, now unhappily deceased, called Mrs Nelson King, the mother of Meriel Forbes (Lady Richardson). I was to receive Four Guineas (less commission) for the week and something for rehearsals, and arrived full of ambition and determination to Make Good.

The theatre was then run by a genial and brilliant director called Gardner Davies, who was married to a charming young lady entitled, unbelievably, Miss Tina Dewsnap. His assistant was Geoffrey Staines, who subsequently ran York Repertory Theatre, one of the foremost in this country. Mr Staines married Pauline Letts, who played for me during two Perranporth seasons after starting her career at Coventry with an abundance of talent. Other members of the company during my stay there were Judy Campbell, John Robinson, James Hayter, someone called Eileen Tingle and a dear little man called Hwfa Pryse (later Hugh Pryse) of such astonishing versatility that he was able to play the title roles in *A Hundred Years Old* and *Young Woodley* on two successive weeks. His death a few years ago robbed the stage of an enchanting personality.

I sucked up like mad to the powers that were during *Clive of India*, and was allowed not only to stay on for the next play (*White Cargo*, as it turned out) but indeed for six months. Looking back, I tend to think of my time at Coventry as 'The Happiest Days of My Career'. Indeed, I honestly believe they were, because I was at that susceptible age when the *camaraderie* and efficiency of a happily united company doing really good work caused great enthusiasm and an inward glow. The standard at this particular theatre was remarkable considering we played twice nightly and changed the play weekly. How the leading players are able to face a new script every Tuesday morning is one of the unsolved mysteries of Repertory. I fear this problem never applied to me, as I was never entrusted with a major role and was indeed given so many 'Butlers' that I eventually bought a morning-suit at Burtons to avoid embarrassment to myself and more especially the costumiers, who were always being asked at the last moment to find clothes to fit my improbable measurements.

In *White Cargo* it was I who had to give the immortal answer to the question 'What, no Cargo?' to which I replied, 'Yes. White Cargo.' (fairly quick curtain). This line had to be delivered in a steady rock-like voice and I was not assisted by what the Ship's Engineer (Mr James Hayter) was a doing of at the time. I was playing the Captain and used to try to avoid looking anywhere near the Ship's E. who, I regret to say, had turned upstage to me by now, displaying to the actors his opened shirt, which disclosed a painted face on his chest with a cigarette, as if by magic, merrily smoking away in his navel. I still think twice before accepting any engagement in any medium if Mr Hayter is anywhere near the cast list, as he is one of the few people who can send me into paroxysms of mirth just by crossing his eyes, as is his wont.

After I had worked myself into becoming a semi-permanent member of the company I relaxed a bit. I was to be paid £4 for the weeks I worked and £2 for the ones when I didn't. I also found myself doing a good deal of cooking for the Messrs Staines and Davies which helped me solidify my position. I lived at a very droll pub called the Smithfield, opposite the theatre, where a lot of the headliners from the variety theatre, the Hippodrome, used to lodge. I was to meet naturally many colourful personalities there, including Nora Williams the Whistling Songstress, an enchanting electric guitarist called Ken Harvey who was mad on electric trains as well, and Larry Adler, who once played 'The Flight of the Bumble Bee' on his harmonica to me in a car outside Kenilworth Castle.

We presented several brand-new plays at Coventry, although none of them got much further. I was in one called *England Expects* which not surprisingly was about Nelson and written by a gentleman called Edgar Middleton, who had previously contributed a jolly sexy play called *Potiphar's Wife*. The Nelson one was very long indeed and not sexy at all. On the Monday night the second house, led by the Mayor of Coventry, staggered wearily away around midnight. Towards the end of a seemingly endless run I suppose I wasn't concentrating as much as I should have been. Anyhow, the line I should have uttered as a sailor aboard the *Victory* was 'The *Leviathan* has been sunk.' I said on this particular occasion, 'The *Lusitania* has been sunk' which seemed to confuse everyone. After the performance a large gentleman came round with my sponsor, Mrs Nelson King, to see us all. Mrs N-K wisely kept her trap shut about her protégé, but the large gent said to me with a sweet smile:

'Yours was, I think, the worst performance I've ever seen on any stage.' It was of course Robert Morley.

He was actually dead right, but I do remember giving a series of excruciating performances while at Coventry. Perhaps the tops in this category was my Old Butler in *March Hares*, though I was treated abominably by the rest of the cast in this production. There was for instance the night when I went to pick up James Hayter's suitcases (usually empty). On this occasion they were practically immobile, as Mr H. had filled them to the brim with stage weights. Later in the week I went deaf in one ear, after bathing in an over-chlorinated swimming-pool, but this unfortunate mishap should not have impelled the company to bellow at me as if I was stone-deaf, which indeed I was after two performances of this sort of thing.

A few weeks later *The Midshipmaid* came sailing over the horizon, in which play I had, for reasons best known to the authors, to play the back legs of a horse during the action. (A pretend-horse, of course.) Now this specialized role is not a comfortable one at the best of times, and as I suffer from claustrophobia I tried to secure the part of the front legs. But it was not to be, and to make matters worse it was midsummer and Front Legs, I regret to report, broke wind during one of the perfs. To light a cigarette INSIDE a horse's skin is a v. difficult operation and I am afraid I lost my temper, hit the bottom of Front Legs, forced him to break into a gallop and we had a blazing row (slightly muffled) which didn't help the audience to follow the plot.

The next week wasn't much better and just as claustrophobic, though less smelly. Actually I had a week-out in theory, but they asked me if I'd mind playing the clock in *Ten Minute Alibi*. If you have seen the play and remember it at all, you will know that the entire plot depends on the rendering and behaviour of The Clock. Some poor person has to stand inside the clock, making the necessary adjustments. I completely lost my head on the first night and moved the hands round twenty minutes instead of the required ten, which immediately rendered the play gibberish and split up a good many Coventry marriages as couples argued their way back after the performance. It could not go on like this and my understudy was put on for the remainder of the week.

I realized my days at Coventry were numbered, and after a not very convincing display as a Glee-Singer in *The Farmer's Wife*, was told regretfully that my engagement was to be terminated. I left the theatre with a lot of presents, some valuable friendships, and a firm conviction that I was not really fitted for repertory work. Many of the company soon established themselves in various fields, and Gardner Davies was to direct many big successes in the West End until his early death (in a tragic fall from the balcony of the Richmond Theatre) cut short a brilliant career.

Back in London I found a lot of assorted work. There were small parts in films and I broke into TV, in those days an exciting and unpredictable medium, far cosier than it is now. But the most important thing that happened was the cementing of an enduring friendship with Robert Morley, who was to exert such an influence on my life. He was and is the wittiest man I know and, although a great many people seem to find him rather frightening, to me his great kindness, generosity and loyalty more than compensate for his unorthodox approach to the Muse.

He was at this time a comparatively unknown actor who had written a first play entitled *Short Story*, which had been accepted by the firm of H.M. Tennent. The cast they procured for this piece included Marie Tempest, Sybil Thorndike, Ursula Jeans, Margaret Rutherford and two young actors called A.E. Matthews and Rex Harrison. So, Mr Morley was sitting fairly pretty, particularly as the director was named Tyrone Guthrie.

But he still rather enjoyed acting in those days and was willing to do anything that cropped up, and there is an endearing story of him walking down Lisle Street (off Leicester Square) in a haze of pleasure, having just fixed a job, when he was accosted by a pretty but rather over-painted member of the feminine sex.

'Doing anything, dear?' she asked.

'Oh yes,' replied Mr Morley, swelling out with pride, 'I'm just going out on tour as a Pirate in *Treasure Island!*'

When I planned my first Perranporth Summer Theatre Season he agreed to come down and act roles as assigned. He was wonderfully co-operative and was persuaded to play the really terrible part of the comic, Tim Bobbin, in *Maria Marten, or Murder in the Red Barn*. This was to be my last production of this season and was not really a happy experiment, though Richard Ainley was pretty spectacular as the dastardly William Corder. Robert was desperately unhappy in his role and I had to give him five shillings a night in order to purchase sweets to bribe the audience into oblivion while he was on. But the ordeal was so soul-shattering to Mr Morley that on the last night of all he gave his entire make-up box, consisting of a stick of five greasepaint, a stick of nine, one powder puff and some pretty sinister crêpe hair to Richard Ainley and announced his immediate resignation from the acting profession. It was no job for a gentleman, he said, and his mother had been right. Henceforth he would write exclusively and not have to prostitute himself.

A few weeks previously he had advised Frith Banbury not to play a part in the Stokes' play on Oscar Wilde which was about to be put on at the Gate Theatre Studio by Norman Marshall. It could only be presented at a theatre of this type as the Lord Chamberlain had banned it. Mr Morley had advised Mr Banbury not on any account to accept the engagement as it would do him irreparable harm to be associated with such a venture and such a play. Mr Banbury listened with great attention and clinched the deal, but I think even Robert was mildly surprised a few weeks later to find himself playing the title role (viz. Oscar Wilde) in that very production. This step was to start him off on his meteoric career, as he made a sensational success in the play, to be repeated a few months later at the Fulton Theatre, New York.

But even this did not prevent him from coming back to Perranporth the following year for the second season and for peanuts (or rather Cornish Cream, as it turned out). He had also found time to write a play specially for the little theatre, *Goodness, How Sad!*, to which we gave a 'World Première' on 26 July 1937. It was directed there by the author and we were all pretty mad about it. Luckily the audiences seemed to share our enthusiasm and I was determined to get it to London as quickly as possible. But there were a lot of snags, mainly financial, to be overcome, and in the middle of our struggles to achieve our desires Robert was invited to Hollywood to make final tests for a film called *Marie Antoinette* in which it was proposed that he should play Louis XVI. It seemed a chance not to be missed, and I saw him off at Waterloo Station rather gloomily. I'm always better at offensive action if someone is there to goad me, and I could see myself drowning the chances of the play in a morass of lethargy and incompetence.

Luckily a few days later I was given an ideal opportunity to procrastinate when the long arm of coincidence stretched out and my phone went with some startling news from the other end of the blower. It was my agents, who rather vaguely inquired if I was interested in making some preliminary tests for a Hollywood film. 'Yes,' I said. 'What film?'

'*Marie Antoinette*,' they replied.

'What part?'

'The King.'

I told them that I had only recently seen the King off on a Southern Railway train and they said they would investigate further.

Later Mr Harold Huth, then in charge of all MGM tests in England, rang me up to tell me that he had received a cryptic cable from California which read, 'Make test of Peter Bull as Gamin.' As he had no script handy and indeed confessed that he had never heard the word 'Gamin' except as applicable to some of Miss Elisabeth Bergner's performances, he was in a slight quandary. I am bound to say that at this period my chances seemed anything but rosy, but somehow I thought it was worth an effortette and darted off to the British Museum, where I had a friend in the Library, who handed me down a lot of heavy tomes about the French Rev. After many hours' study I elucidated the undoubted fact that Gamin was Louis XVI's rather common blacksmith friend, who poisoned people on the side. It wasn't much of a help really, as he appeared to be rather a shadowy figure. However, I reported my findings to Mr Huth, who said he would test me and perhaps I would like to write the script. Now this was quite a turn-up for the book, as very few people, except Emlyn W, N. Coward and Mr Morley are allowed to say what they write, and I knew for a fact that Mr Morley on this occasion had had to say Other People's Lines, so I basked in my luck and tore off a very showy little scene with no other characters. It was difficult to do and I made myself go a bit potty at the end to help the viewer, and Mr Huth directed me with sympathy and understanding. I did the test at Elstree where the studios for the past few months had been littered with Louis XVIs of various distinctions and one King of France had actually bumped into another in the corridor. But I was relieved to find no sign of another Gamin, did my lot and disappeared back to London. For months I heard nothing, although later it transpired that my test, and that of the late Francis L. Sullivan (as Louis XVI), had come down in an aeroplane in the middle of the Arizona desert. I hung on as long as I could, encouraged by long letters from Robert saying how excruciatingly funny it was out there, but finally had to set about getting work of some sort.

I still couldn't raise the capital for *Goodness, How Sad!*, and was suddenly asked by Norman Marshall to compère his annual Gate Theatre Studio revue. These were very chic affairs, starring Hermione Gingold, whose immense talents were then apparently only recognized by the faithful habitués of the tiny theatre. It sounded an exciting idea and I was keen to do it. Reginald Beckwith and my oldest friend in the world, Nicholas Phipps, were writing most of the material, and it was proposed that I should wander on and off dressed as Father Time and have terrible rows with J.B. Priestley (to be played by Beckwith) about being tampered with. It must be explained that 1937 was the year when Priestley had two big successes on in London, called *Time and the Conways* and *I Have been Here Before*, both of which dealt with the time factor.

A very amusing company had been engaged and I was really rather looking forward to it all, but in some obscure way could not believe that I would ever actually open in the revue. So I was not altogether surprised when my agent, the late Vere Barker, summoned me during rehearsals and drove me in his black Rolls to the MGM office in Lower Regent Street. Here Mr Ben Goetz received us in most friendly fashion and was unwise enough to leave the room for a few seconds during the interview. It was thus easy for my long-sighted eyes to read the cable which lay on the desk and read quite simply: 'Get Bull on next boat.' I was in consequence very over-excited, but Mr Barker managed to be sufficiently off-hand with Mr Goetz on his return to make my blood curdle but to secure for me a splendid and generous contract.

Mr Marshall and the cast of the revue forgave me and I left almost immediately on the *Normandie*, I mean *in* the *Normandie*, where of course I won the table-tennis competition, beating M. Charles Boyer in the opening round. I finished the voyage in a coma of good living and was not sick once. As Bob Ritchie, Jeanette Macdonald's then current husband and Mr Goetz's right-hand man, had pointed out to me, 'Ben Goetz is practically king of the *Normandie*', which indeed was proved by the accommodation provided. On arrival at New York I was met by a posse of gents from Metro-Goldwyn Mayer, who were slightly taken aback by my old trunk exploding as it descended the chute in the Customs Yard. However they shepherded me about New York during the day, and I had tea with Mr and Mrs Charles B. Cochran, and left for California by air that evening. I was met at the airport by R. Morley and Llewellyn Rees. The latter, who had just finished an engagement with *George and Margaret* in New York, had decided to stay on in America and had unwisely said he would be our chauffeur and companion in Hollywood during the winter months. He put up with a good deal of sauce from us both, and our general behaviour both at the dinner and the card table left a certain amount to be desired.

Mr Morley was wearing a nice blue sports jacket; not, you may think, a very sensational bit of information to convey to you, but I would point out that I was disporting its twin, having bought the only possible coat (figuratively speaking) remaining on Simpsons' pegs. We hurriedly came to an arrangement to wear The Coat on alternate days, and it did enable us to play patch-as-patch-can when they got ragged.

The Messrs Morley and Rees had installed themselves in a flat in Westwood Village, which was then a tiny suburb of Beverly Hills, and had taken a jolly nice little one for me almost next door. We had a fairly eccentric Filipino servant who cooked dreamily beautiful rice dishes and gave notice once a week. He was called Sammy and remained in our employment throughout our stay. The film had apparently not even started, and after the first day we didn't go near the studio for a bit. I had lunch there and got enough thrills to last me for quite a time. At the centre table in the MGM commissariat were the Messrs Gable, Tracy, Powell, a lot of Barrymores and the Mesdames Lamarr, Loy and Macdonald, and as Robert had been given Garbo's old dressing-room, I was able to bask on the famous lavatory seat to my heart's content.

In the afternoon, wandering around the huge MGM Empire with my agent, I ran into a tall lanky gent with a fairly extensive vocabulary, who ended a long monologue to what turned out to be *our* agent, with a telling phrase addressed to me: 'Oh, they've got you in the prison now, have they?' After he'd gone I asked my *agent-*

provocateur who he was. 'That's Noel Langley,' he replied. 'I don't think he likes it here.' Like it he didn't in those days, we discovered, and made no bones about it. He was cursing a good deal at having to write scripts for Macdonald and Eddy, wrote smashing ones for *The Wizard of Oz* and *Maytime*, and with his ravishing South African wife made splendid company and handed out a lot of laughs. We were to be associated on and off for many years, though 'off' was the more frequent association. After my day in the studio I was told to relax for a bit, and so we settled down for a good many games of Monopoly (the American version with Park Avenue instead of Park Lane). We changed later to a snobby game called 'High Society', the aim of which was to collect as many Social Points as possible. One could get houses in Florida, yachts, polo ponies and a camp in the Adirondacks (whatever that could be), but you lost a lot of Social Points if your daughter married a bogus count, the chauffeur or, I imagine, a camp in the Adirondacks.

We didn't play these games entirely by ourselves because, apart from the Langleys, we got to know other expatriates like ourselves. The literary critic of the *Observer*, John Davenport, was an amusing companion who was almost as bad a loser at Monopoly as Robert and me and, I regret to report, once upset the board ON PURPOSE. Then there was Mary Morris, a young actress with beautiful eyes and great integrity, who came out on an idiot's contract of seventy-five dollars a week or thereabouts, which made living pretty difficult. The Studios could not think what to do with her, as she comformed not at all to any preconceived idea of a Film Actress, and used to test her bi-weekly in improbable costumes. One would meet her on a Monday wandering gloomily round the lot dressed as a French courtesan at the court of Louis the something, and on the Thursday she'd be portraying a very blacked-up servant from the deep, deep South. As she also had to attend acting classes and the gymnasium, she got very unhappy indeed and eventually got her release, which resulted in an enormous personal success for her in a film called *Prison without Bars* made in England. She did ask to be routed back from Hollywood via Siberia, which shook the Travel Department a bit.

But that was all much later, and anyhow the Metro-Goldwyn-Mayer set-up was so wrapt in mystery, intrigue and curious carryings-on that one never quite knew where one was. *Marie Antoinette* was to pass through many hands. When I first arrived out there a gentleman called Sydney Franklin, who had done several years' research on the subject, was supposed to direct it, but I think he wanted to spend rather a long time on it which didn't quite fit in with a sudden economy campaign at the studio, so the job was switched to 'Woody' Van Dyke, the splendid director of *The Thin Man* series who, I am pretty sure, thought a Dauphin was a large fish. Anyhow, Mr Franklin, who had soaked himself in Versailles lore, was carried away to a nursing-home and that was that.

Mr Hunt Stromberg was the producer, and I was summoned to his office quite early on and told of many startling future plans for me, but the immediate ones concerned my learning the American tongue in order to play the French blacksmith. I had an hour every day with a nice lady who turned out to be of Swedish extraction, but she made me promise not to tell. I never asked why I had to speak American, but in a way I was relieved, as lines like 'Now you're sore at me' (addressed to Louis XVI of France) are not easy to say in any other language. Actually I did make the error of complaining about this very line, which resulted in a midget script conference and a new line: 'Now you're mad at me.'

Depicting the title role was Miss Norma Shearer, whose come-back this was to be. I believe at that time she owned fifty-one per cent of the shares of MGM (bequeathed by her late husband Irving Thalberg), so I watched with fascination to see how she was treated. I found her enchanting and was delighted by the string quartette that she had on the set between 'takes'. I was also enormously impressed by her technique, though I fear she was very unhappy in her role. Others in the cast were Tyrone Power, John Barrymore, Gladys George, Joseph Schildkraut and Robert Morley. Robert was meant to support her but he didn't really. He just walked away with the film, a remarkable achievement for an actor whose only previous experience of the Bioscope was being sacked from *Under the Red Robe* at Denham Studios, England. It was an astonishing début, and his method of acting foxed the Hollywood habitués considerably.

Most of my scenes were with him and were not directed by Van Dyke who had to deal with all the Shearer scenes. But by this time, looking down their lists, MGM had discovered that they had Julien Duvivier, the great French director under contract and doing damn all. He had been brought over to remake *Pepé Le Moko* which was eventually done catastrophically by another studio. So poor M. Duvivier directed crowd and odd scenes in *Marie and Toilette* as Robert now called it. He seemed fairly dispirited and with reason.

I had two days' work in the first two months, and was exhausted when it came to the big revolutionary scenes in Versailles where the mob were to break in. We had been warned that there was going to be plenty of action, but I was a bit alarmed by the number of nurses in attendance. I later discovered that the Palace Guards had signed away their persons for bags of gold, or rather the stunt men playing the Palace Guards had. Robert and I were fairly windy and not looking forward to this sequence at all. I suddenly noticed among the crowd a large gentleman dressed exactly like me. I immediately suspected, frankly not without cause, that I had been replaced in the role of Gamin without being myself advised of the change. I went up to him and exchanged the following bizarre intercourse:

'Good morning,' I said.

'Morning,' he replied civilly.

'Got a good part?' I inquired cautiously.

'Doing the dangerous bits for you.'

I was nonplussed.

'Do you do a lot of this kind of work?' I asked.

'Yeah,' he said. 'I was one of the apes in *Tarzan*.'

This was a real conversation-stopper and I edged away. Later on, when I was bruised all over and had broken a bone in my elbow, I meant to ask him how he had fared; but I never saw him again. Perhaps he was a mirage. The mob were pretty tough, and we all came in for some rough handling. There was also a horrid scene when I was stabbed in the back by Barry Fitzgerald. In order to make this frightfully convincing, I was given small bags of chocolate sauce to bite on at the crucial moment, so that it spurted attractively out of my trap. We had just the twenty-eight takes on this one, and I didn't eat chocolates for twenty-eight months at least. The monotony of the scene and the unpleasantness of treading on a chocolate-caked carpet brought on an intense nausea, not helped by a too realistic copy of Miss Anita Louise's head (she was playing the Princesse de Lamballe) whizzing past the fairly French windows on a pike.

At the end of this sequence I was told I would not be needed for some time, so that I could settle down and get accustomed to life in Hollywood. This was a disheartening period and I could find no reality of any sort in the surroundings. Everyone there seemed at this time to be only interested in the film industry, and the newspapers were exclusively devoted to film news and it was frightening to see how far this self-abuse was carried. I read in one paper that 'Peter Bull, the hefty British actor, is disappointed at the size of the swimming-pools in Hollywood,' which item of absorbing significance was only one in a series of inanities about me.

Robert and I got pretty bored, and the games of chance as played in the home were getting more and more acrimonious, so we took to driving down to town and going into a sports shop where we twiddled a roulette wheel at fifty dollars a whack, which shook Llewellyn Rees so much that he confiscated our pocket-money and kept us very short indeed. We went to the pictures a bit, and they used to have 'sneak previews' in our local cinema. One night we wandered down there, and there seemed to be a considerable *brouhaha* in progress. A new film from our own studio was to be shown that evening and we were recognized by one of our pressmen and asked to say a few words into the mike to the listening millions. We were delighted to do so, and after delivering some sparkling dialogue we adjourned to the box-office, where we had the humiliating experience of being refused admission for the silly reason that no one had provided us with tickets. So back to Monopoly in the sanctity of the home.

The rainy season was quite funny. As California refuses to admit that it can rain much there, there are the minimum of gutters and drains to get rid of the stuff when it arrives. We had several days of cloudbursts and driving rain, and there were consequently floods and even the studios were under water. Hysterical voices on the radio told us to say in our homes (more Monopoly) and that some Great Dam was coming unstuck, but we heeded not and waded out in order to see the dinghies and other craft that enterprising persons were sailing up and down Hollywood Boulevard.

The weeks rolled by, until one day I realized that I had saved enough money to have a bash at putting on *Goodness, How Sad!* in London. Later on there was to be a headline in the *Daily Express* which read: FOUR DAYS IN FILM PUTS ON WEST-END PLAY, a statement which was technically correct but did not best please my ex-employers. But the fact remains that I was still being kept in Hollywood, albeit on full salary, but with no likelihood of working again. They kept burbling about possible re-takes, but as they had never taken very much (of me) in the first place, it seemed a fantasy. Just as I had made up my mind to lie back and become one of Hollywood's Forgotten Men, they told me I could go. I decided to travel across America in a puff-puff, and took a ticket on the most glamorous puff-puff in the US, called the Super-Chief. Llewellyn came to see me off, and Robert, to my surprise, arrived just as the guard was waving the train out of the station. I had last seen him going to the studio to work but he told me that he'd been sent to inform me that I would after all be needed for re-takes.

I was almost taken in by his performance, but wisely decided to risk it and spent a pretty boring four days getting across America. I had a night in New York at the end of it, which I spent viewing Thornton Wilder's enchanting play *Our Town*. The next day I sailed in the *Aquitania* for England, in which ship I of course won the table-tennis championship. I was horrified, though, to discover that the cup presented by the British ship does not respond to Silver-Dip (Advt), whereas its French comrade does. Still, I am the only actor in the world to have won the Blue Riband of the Atlantic for Ping-Pong. So there!

I suppose it's out of character for me to end a chapter in a blaze of glory, so I'd better insert my postscript now and not put it in 'Addenda'. I was cut clean out of the Metro-Goldwyn-Mayer

Production of *Marie Antoinette*, but I did get my shoulders into one of the stills outside the Empire Cinema, the result of six months well and usefully spent.

3
A Slight Case of Mismanagement

Back in London I set about going into management with *Goodness, How Sad!* Before Robert and I left for Hollywood we had exhausted every Avenue of Possibility and had been nowhere near able to get into the Shaftesbury one. In fact, we had been driven to considering seriously such unlikely theatres as The Little Theatre and the Lyric, Hammersmith. The former used to be perched precariously behind the Tivoli Cinema, though now both places of entertainment have disappeared, and so perhaps I had better describe it as a hundred yards due south of the Adelphi. Anyhow, we were offered the theatre for forty pounds a week, which may seem to you a more than reasonable rent for a West-End theatre, but not when I tell you that at this period the whole of the street outside the Little was cut off from traffic owing to demolition of property. It would have involved our patrons walking quite a way, to say nothing of the artistes, and although it was a dear little theatre in its heyday it was a bit off the beaten track; though I suppose we could have advertised it as being very much on the beaten track, as the noise from the electric drills would have deafened audience and actors alike.

At this time we had very limited capital and I had been unable to raise any more. One of the disadvantages of the poor going into management is that they have to ask people for money and I am not at all good at this. It was the same problem when I was an advertising canvasser, simply because I have never had the confidence to convince would-be investors that they would even get their money back, much less make a small fortune. However, with my pockets bulging with American dollars, I felt quite differently on my return from Hollywood.

I formed myself into a limited liability company, called for some obscure reason, Peter Bull Ltd. It is, I think, one of the few businesses extant which have actually held an Annual General Meeting in the sea. It was terribly hot at the time and seemed the best place. Having read company law, I was determined on one occasion to hold an AGM in a lift; I had gathered that it would have to be stationary the whole time in order to follow correct procedure, but some silly ass kept on wanting to use the damned thing just as the Sec. was reading the minutes.

The extraordinary thing about the affairs of Peter Bull Ltd is, that though we started off merry as grigs with £2,000 in the bank, since then we never seem to have more than 16s.3d. and I always have to pop something in when 'Charges' are due. It's worrying because, although I have lost my all twice in management or mismanagement, I am still fascinated by it and the urge might seize me again at any moment and 16s. 3d. is not really sufficient to put on a distinguished production, even if the entertainment-tax burden has been raised. I suppose at a pinch we could do *Waiting for Godot*, which only needs a bare stage and a tree which has no leaves, but that play always leads to unpleasantness, as you will see later on.

Peter Bull Ltd started off by being quite a family party. The shareholders (or debenture-holders as they were saucily called) were my brother Anthony, Robert Morley, Hugh Sinclair, Mr Hayes-Hunter (the author's agent), Gerald Savory, a friend of Frith Banbury (called, I think, Alan Roger) and Mrs Gordon Latta who had been with me in *Escape Me Never*. I put in slightly more than anyone else in order to inspire a bit of faith.

While the company was being formed, Robert Morley disappeared to New York to repeat his triumph in *Oscar Wilde*, which was just as well, as I don't think he would have enjoyed my subsequent machinations to keep all our heads above water. He did, however, help very greatly with the casting and above all persuade Tyrone Guthrie to direct the piece.

Available theatres were still pretty scarce in spite of the damping

effect of the Munich crisis, but by a stroke of luck I was able to secure the Vaudeville Theatre owing to a rather macabre state of affairs. A couple of young men from Yorkshire called Schofield had taken a lease of the theatre and, flushed with enthusiasm, had announced that the Vaudeville would be 'The House of Comedy'. As an opening attraction they put on a play by Val Gielgud, starring the late Ronald Squire, but the piece did not 'catch the public fancy' and closed in a very short time. They were caught with no follow-up and inserted a revival of *Ghosts* with Marie Ney, which was highly praised but did not quite fit in with the theatre's new policy.

As a result, when I made my bid they were not unpleased to consider a proposition. I got it fairly cheaply (£150 a week and four weeks' rent in advance) and then could go ahead with contracts, etc. The nucleus of the Perranporth production was to be preserved intact, and Roger Furse was to reproduce his superb dingy-digs set. Of the original company Judith Furse and Frith Banbury were to play their original roles, and as the parts had been written for them they could not have been bettered. Pauline Letts, who had created the part of Carol the young actress round whom the play revolved, was no longer available, as by this time she was a wife and mother and showing a zest for domesticity and bringing up enchanting children which was to play havoc with her stage career. I am happy to report that she is back in harness now that domestic demands have eased. In her place we engaged a young girl called Jill Furse (a cousin of Roger and Judith). She was an actress of immense sensitivity and appeal who died at the beginning of the war. Her engagement in the piece made the Furse element so strong that one critic was to head his notice: 'Goodness, How Furse!'

I martyred myself by NOT again playing Herr Angst, the gentleman with the performing seals, an act of sacrifice, as I adored the part but thought it wiser not to run the risk of making a muck of both my managerial and Thespian careers in 'one foul sweep' as my mother has been heard to say. The late Arthur Hambling played the part superbly and Kathleen Boutall was enormously funny as his wife, dressed at one stage of the play in a little girl's sailor-suit. To play the important part of Mrs Priskin, the frightening landlady, we got Mary

Merrall, who had rarely played comedy before and who started a new career for herself as the result of her big success.

But the most serious problem was who should play Robert Maine, the film star with whom the young actress falls in love. A lot of stars would not touch it because the part did not appear in the last scene and anyhow required a certain amount of unselfishness, and we were incredibly lucky to persuade Hugh Sinclair, then on the crest of a wave as a leading-man in films and the theatre, to play it. He contributed a charming and valuable performance, and by his experience and skill was able to help the younger members of the cast. He is always wonderfully unselfish where young people are concerned, and few people who saw *Claudia* will forget the support he lent to Pamela Brown in her first starring part.

For the remainder of the set-up I was in safe and friendly hands. Margaret Fraser, a tower of strength from Perranporth, was to help the stage management, and Llewellyn Rees was to be my manager and steer me through innumerable nasty moments. It is entirely due to Mr Rees that I was not submerged in debt and disaster. In charge of publicity was a very original lady called Mrs Peggy Laing, who also handled the Windmill Theatre, assisted by a young lady of immense *joie de vivre* called Sheila Van Damm. Their method with press people was fairly unorthodox and, in Peggy's case, usually consisted of phrases like: 'There's a ghastly little play coming on which I don't suppose you want to do anything about' or 'Aren't these photographs dreary? You can't possibly want to use them': an approach which was so original that she practically always got what she wanted.

And there we were, all ready to go. After paying the rent for four weeks, I sat back and quite frankly enjoyed the whole thing. Rehearsals went more than smoothly and there were no rows and no temperaments. I was a little surprised that there was no advance booking, but the first night looked healthy. I got the curtain up for £1,200, which left £800 for emergencies, of which there were to be plenty. But everyone seemed to wish us well and *What's On* published a picture of me affirming that I was 'the youngest manager in London'. I let the capable box-office gentleman deal with the first-night applications and put everyone in their place. I did manage to persuade Elisabeth Bergner to come in a box, no mean achievement, as she loathed publicity or social functions of any sort. I left some flowers and a few indoor games in the box, in case she and Margaret Kennedy, who accompanied her, got bored. In other boxes the Furse parents (Sir William and Lady) faced the Bull parent (Lady) across the theatre and I popped assorted Bulls in other boxes. Dotted all over the house were a vast assortment of friends and well-wishers from Perranporth and I had no qualms at all until my white stiff shirt refused to co-operate, broke the studs and burst open to expose most of my torso, and I had to spend the rest of the evening with a scarf round my neck, which certainly didn't qualify me for the role of 'London's best-dressed manager'. Luckily this occurred after being photographed with Miss Bergner arriving at the theatre and, as usual, being described as 'Peter Ball' in one of the papers the next day.

Anyhow this was only a small fly in the ointment that evening, as the play went extremely well and even better than one had dared to hope. At the end there were cheers, and the reception was so enthusiastic that Hugh made a speech of thanks and told the audience that he would cable the author immediately, informing him of their delightful reaction. Later the most famous critic of the day, the late Mr James Agate, told Hugh to include his name in the cable, which sent all our spirits sky-high. This was at a party given in Roger Furse's studio after the first night, where we all adjourned and celebrated the evening in riotous fashion.

I was up at dawn to get the papers and found that they were unanimous in their approval, though several commented unfavourably on the title which still seems to me the perfect one for this play. But the general tone of the notices was very enthusiastic and I could easily see that we had our pick of quotable bits to display all over London.

'Gladness, How Good' (*Daily Sketch*)
'Gladdens the heart' (*Daily Express*)
'Delightful Evening's Entertainment' (*Daily Mail*)

And the 'Sundays' were to prove even better for advertising purposes:

> 'Another *French Without Tears*' (*Sunday Express*)
> 'One long laugh' (*Sunday Pictorial*)
> 'One of the most entertaining plays for months'
> (*Sunday Dispatch*)

But £28 5s.8d. did not seem an adequate reward, and this is the figure to which we played on the second night. On the other hand my mother, a shrewd critic, had made two rather pertinent observations on the phone that morning.

'I enjoyed it very much, dear,' she said, 'but it's a pity that Jill Furse wears such dowdy clothes and there are no changes of scene. The digs are a bit depressing.'

It was no good assuring her that repertory actresses do have to wear dowdy clothes and keep their best for the stage and that digs are depressing. It is just that the ordinary audience believe that the whole of the stage must be tinged with glamour and very few of them can even imagine what life in the lower registers of the profession really means.

However, we cheered up at the thought of what James Agate was going to say on Sunday, and as a large section of the public followed his advice implicitly, we hung on to our hats. We went up seven pounds on the Thursday and Friday nights and got into three figures for the Saturday – but only just. Even with the first night we had only played to £368 on the six performances.

You can imagine our disappointment when we tore through the theatre columns of the *Sunday Times* and found that Mr Agate had dismissed *Goodness, How Sad!* more than lightly, describing it as a 'pretty minoperative' play, which was not exactly calculated to send the customers helter-skelter down the Strand. But it was the space that he devoted to his notice which was so humiliating. There were less than a dozen lines in all, culminating in the cast list, headed by the phrase: 'the piece was acted for all it's worth by', and though this did not lead to any jealousy on the part of the artistes, it was a tremendous let-down. None of us would have minded if he had not gone so far in his praise verbally, after the first performance.

After we had lost over £200 on each of the two successive weeks, it was obvious that drastic steps would have to be taken. The takings were only just over £400 a week and the vast resources of P. Bull Ltd were exhausted. And this was despite Robert Morley forgoing his royalties and Hugh Sinclair (the only remotely well-paid member of the company) popping in his cheques very belatedly. First I went to the brothers Schofield and told them I could not continue to present the play at their theatre under these circumstances. They agreed generously to let me have it at a greatly reduced rent (£60 a week, in fact, though with a large increase in percentage over a certain takings' figure), and I had then to go to the cast and ask them to accept cuts in their already pretty parlous salaries. They were magnanimous and co-operative, and as a result of these negotiations I was able to get the 'get-out' figure down to £500 a week.

I then went on an all-out campaign to bully people into coming to see the play. Friends, actors and relatives were given thousands of throwaways eulogizing the piece, to leave about in buses, tubes and taxis. Restaurants were flooded with the damned things and Miss Valerie Taylor (Hugh Sinclair's wife at the time) was caught by her manager (Mr Beaumont of H.M. Tennent) distributing handbills to the enormous queues wanting to see her in *Call It a Day*. Mr Beaumont, justifiably, I think, asked her to desist.

I rang up James Agate bravely and was dismissed with a flea in my ear, when he said he could not return to a play he had already reviewed, but the late Sydney Carroll sprung to our assistance. He was then the theatrical correspondent of the *Daily Telegraph* and devoted a long article to one particular play every Thursday. In response to my appeal he picked out *Goodness, How Sad!* which had an immediate though minuscule effect on the box-office. We rose to slightly below £500 on the following week. But until Christmas we never had a profit-making week, which was maddening, as those who came were very appreciative and even the great Charles B. Cochran wrote me an ecstatic letter which I had photostated and put outside the front of the theatre.

The curious part about it all is that I never thought of taking it off or that it would ever play to such a catastrophic week that it would plunge Peter Bull Ltd into bankruptcy. At the end of January 1939, we got associated with that pernicious system known as 'twofers', by which customers could have two seats for the price of one by presenting a card which showed that they had paid a very small sum to an organization called the Privilege Ticket Register. It was a constant embarrassment to me to watch a nice customer amble up to the box office and buy two expensive stalls for 27s., only to be followed by a 'twofer' lady who got the same thing for 13s. 6d. But it did increase the intake by a little and we were able to coast into the spring. But by March we had reached the end of our reserves, though by selling the film rights to Ealing films, we were able to put some money back into the company.

At the end of March Hugh Sinclair and Jill Furse left the cast to make a bit of money in films (and who could blame them?), and I was lucky to get Sebastian Shaw and Jenny Laird to replace them. They were excellent, and continued in the play until the run ended on 6 May 1939, having achieved 237 performances.

The only people who did remotely well out of it financially were Guthrie, who had directed it superbly for a minute basic fee but then went on a percentage, and Roger Furse, who had designed the set for love and, I am ashamed to admit, £15 and a tiny percentage. For the company it must be said that the play made the reputations of all those actors who had none at the commencement, and the management glowed with the record of an eight months' run as a first venture.

The last week we played to a very cool £320, but, to cheer us up, dear Robert Morley, who had made less than anyone on the production, in spite of his authorship, sent us a large sum of money to have an outing on the first Monday after we had closed. So off we set to a splendid tuck-in across the road from the stage door at Rules Restaurant, where a special menu (headed 'In Memoriam *Goodness, How Sad!*) was given to us and then we all went, with our wives or whatever we had with us at the time, to see Herbert Farjeon's lovely revue *Nine Sharp* at the Little Theatre.

And that was that. I felt no remorse or bitterness about the play, as it could not be classed as a failure in the ordinary sense. Both the press and the public liked it, but as it has never done well since, either on tour or in the repertory theatres, I can only guess that it lacks popular appeal. But it will always be revived as it is a remarkably true and honest play, which provides splendid parts for actors who can for a change understand what they are talking about. It has some touching stuff, as when the young actress turns on the film star who has said he won't help them by appearing in their dying 'rep':

CAROL: We listened to you and now it's our turn. We're the theatre, see! You may have forgotten what that is, but I'll remind you. It's the place where you learned your job, which cradled you, which gave you your first chance, which made an actor out of you, which sent you to Hollywood to make pictures. And just because you don't need us any more you think you can walk out on us … well, you can't. You've got a debt to pay, Robert Maine, and you're not going to get away without paying it! It's a big debt too. You're happy now, you're rich, you're doing what you like, you're proud of yourself. Well, everything you've got you owe to us. There wouldn't be any pictures at all if it wasn't for the theatre. The theatre, that's something bigger than anything you'll ever know in Hollywood, something that was going hundreds of years before the cinema was ever heard of, and you know and I know it will be going on thousands of years after motion pictures are dead and buried. The greatest author that ever lived once described the whole thing in five words, 'All The World's a Stage.'

To which the poor film star can only reply: 'Have a glass of water.' And the observation throughout is so acute. Listen to the little scene where the two girls in the company are reading the eagerly awaited notice in the local paper:

CAROL: Here we are. 'Amusements'.
CHRISTINE: That's something, anyway.

CAROL: 'Sea Lions at the Hippodrome'. Why do they always put the Hippodrome before us?

CHRISTINE: Their advertisement is bigger.

CAROL: 'The Repertory Company at the Opera House is presenting *When in Rome* this week. This is a smart and witty comedy well suited to the talented company. Mr Osbert Faith is convincing as the Father, while Miss Carol Sands scores heavily as Millicent. Mr Peter Thropp makes use of his rich comic opportunities and mention must be made of Miss Christine Lawford as a maid. The settings by Arthur Hardy are excellent, and Mr Lambert is the popular front of the house manager.'

Why do they bother to put that in each week?

CHRISTINE: Mr Lambert writes the notice himself, I imagine.

It seems to me that there in a tiny scene is reflected all the heartbreak and comedy of the theatrical profession. But I must not quote any more from this (to me) entrancing play, and I leave it with the regret that it obviously cannot be everyone's cup of tea.

It was now nearly summer 1939 and full of fresh hopes and enthusiasm, a lot of us went down to Perranporth for what was to prove the last season of the Summer Theatre. I had a brand new play by Noel Langley, called *The Walrus and the Carpenter*, with which I hoped to recoup my losses, and an exceptionally strong company, which included Miss Pamela Brown, a lot of Furses and Mr Robert Morley. But on 3 September 1939, we had to close the theatre owing to circumstances over which we had no control, and we all ended up in some very peculiar places.

PART TWO

To Sea in a Sieve

4
Anzio, Anzio, Anzio

By January 1944 I had become, through a bewildering series of misadventures, Commander of His Majesty's Landing Craft Flak 16[1], one of an unbroken line of Allied Craft which stretched the entire length of the port of Messina, Sicily.

Rumours of an approaching operation against Anzio were current, but the Squadron Commander thought it more likely that we should be sent to Bari, on the east coast of Italy, for harbour defence duties. In any case, I could see no objective for a fresh landing in Italy; on the west coast there were incomparable facilities at Naples for unloading supplies to the front line, and on the other side Bari appeared on the face of it more than adequate. But in Combined Operations all things were possible, and I heaved a sigh of relief when Flak 16 got its sailing orders for Bari. These were promptly cancelled.

Our sudden inclusion in the new operation was due to the fact that one of the Flaks scheduled for it had engine defects. We were rapidly sailed to Naples. Here were all the signs of chaotic preparation that usually preceded a 'do'. We had no sooner stored and ammunitioned the ship than we adjourned to Salerno for our final instructions. The little town looked remarkably quiet and ordered, and it was astonishing to realize that only four months ago it had been the centre of some of the bloodiest fighting in the campaign. The briefing was clear and concise until I was handed about a thousand pages of material of which thirty affected me. In actual fact I could find no trace of a mention of Flak 16 in the orders

[1] Anti-aircraft Landing vessel

or even of the ship we had replaced, and in theory I should have stayed cosily at home. But out of the welter of information received I could see the point of the operation.

We were to land troops, etc., at the small watering-place of Anzio, which was a popular holiday resort for Romans, being only twenty miles distant from the capital. The invasion was intended to relieve pressure on the Cassino front and render Rome immediately accessible. It all looked fine on paper, and for once I did not see quite as much cause for alarm as usual. The Americans were joining us, and with the close proximity of Naples with its airfields and supplies, it appeared on the surface to hold every hope of success.

We sailed on a moonless but beautiful night on 20 January 1944, in sublime ignorance of the ordeal ahead of us. Priest's[2] customary eve of invasion *bon mot* concerned two islands we passed to port on our way.

'Do those islands belong to us, sir?' he asked.

I had not thought of it before, and although I replied in the affirmative, I realized that time alone would tell. However, they were to prove the least of our worries.

At dawn on the 22nd we lay a mile and half off the coast. The Rocket ships had already done their fabulous stuff, and through the smoke the landing craft were weaving their way in to the beaches. It was an astounding morning, because there was little or no sign of enemy activity; we could see, farther up the coast, spasmodic shelling of minesweepers near the port of Rome, but our sector was subdued and unsensational. I recall very few enemy aircraft the first day, and we hugged ourselves with delight. It was plain that the enemy had been taken by surprise, and we fondly imagined that our troops were by now requisitioning the Colosseum for T. Trinder. It was not until later that we learned that instead of pressing on, the troops had been ordered to entrench themselves strongly to avoid another possible Salerno. I am not enough of a strategist or tactician to discuss the rights and wrongs of this policy, and nothing could be easier than criticism even from an unsafe distance, but when I heard several weeks later that we had advanced just the three miles, I was flabbergasted. But we had surprised the enemy and now it was their turn to surprise us.

I had the Flotilla Officer with me, which always hampered my movements, and meant there was less to eat in the wardroom, two results which irritated me. Yet on 22 January I was in such a good temper that nothing worried me, and I waved cheerfully to my LCT[3] chums as they passed us in an endless stream. We had stationed ourselves about a thousand yards from the shore, where we had a splendid view of the proceedings. At dusk there were several Red Warnings, but nothing of serious import occurred. At 03.00 the following morning we were told to carry out anti-E-boat patrol, which I did without the foggiest notion of what we would do if we saw one except go into reverse screaming for help.

The day was uneventful, but at first signs of nightfall there was a severe dive-bombing attack on two destroyers a mile or so out to sea. A direct hit was scored on one and the ship sank in a few seconds. It gives me a certain twinge of pride to record that we shot down one of the bastards who had done it. It was a Dornier 217, and this time I made no mistake in my claim, as I noted every small detail, and their Lordships acknowledged our kill. That night we carried out our anti-E-boat patrol as if we were the latest cruiser.

On 24 January we were instructed to accompany some Liberty Ships to the other side of the harbour, and at noon we anchored close to the port entrance. It was at this time that the Flotilla Officer said he would look after the ship if I would like to have a lie-down. I had had very little sleep since sailing and accepted his offer with alacrity. There was a light breeze, and I asked him to let me know if anything funny happened. Our senses of humour must have been strangely divergent, as when I reappeared on the bridge four hours later we were chugging slowly past Nettuno, a couple of miles from our starting position. I told them to pull in the anchor, which did not astonish me by its non-appearance. Loss of this commodity always presaged disaster near at hand, and this occasion was no exception. I

[3] Landing Craft Tank

moved to a slightly more sheltered spot and dropped my spare anchor. This held for twenty-four hours, when I noticed that we were once more dragging.

At 23.30 on the 25th our tribulations started. All the familiar storm signs were starting, the hissing through the mast, the frenzied movement on the top of the sea and the sickening feeling at the pit of my stomach. But worse was in store: on starting up the engines Sandy reported that the port engine was useless and I could only have the other for the time being. This was a real problem, since it meant that I could not turn to starboard, as there was an on-shore wind. The engine which was operating had a strong bias to port, and even with the wheel hard over the other way it made no difference. However, I managed to clear the harbour, but I could not make my way to the open sea; craft other than those with stores, etc., on board had been forbidden to use the port for shelter, and the elaborate instructions detailed at length in the operation orders were quite impracticable. We were slowly being carried over to the southern sector, where enemy interference had just started to become tiresome. Shells were reaching the beaches and the ships lying offshore, and I suddenly saw an LST[4] go up in flames. As we were drifting towards her our position was desperate. I knew that a heavily ammunitioned ship like ours would only need a burning fragment to touch something off, and yet, however I manoeuvred, I simply could not turn the craft. Within two hundred yards of the burning hulk I said in a soft voice: 'Please, God, make her turn to starboard.' I said it three times, and then yelled down the voice-pipe: 'Hard to starboard, emergency full speed starboard engine.' I rang the bell to the engine room, which informed Sandy of conditions, and against every rule of navigation, engineering and nature HMLCF 16 turned to starboard and a few hours later the other engine started.

The next morning was a repetition in miniature of the aftermath of the Salerno storm, except that owing to the harbour's protection casualties were far fewer. At least a dozen ships had lost their anchors and the damage in the small craft section was heavy. The

[4] Landing Ships Tank

LST which had been hit showed only her mast above water, and there was a strange atmosphere over the entire beach-head. Although heavy seas were still breaking all over us, it was easier in daylight to cope with the movements of the ship, but it meant a further twenty-hour hours' cruising, as I did not dare drop my little bower anchor. That evening there were more dive-bomb raids and an enemy plane crashed in flames fifty yards from the ship. The seas did not flatten until the morning of the 27th, and the harm was now done.

The unloading had been seriously interrupted, and the Germans had had plenty of time to assemble their reserves and heavy guns. From the Alban Hills they had a clear view of the goings-on, and they brought up a great horror called 'Anzio Annie'. She was a mobile gun who made several appearances every day and dropped charming notes in and around the harbour. She remained in action for over two months and seemed impossible to locate. In spite of the fact that warships and gun-ships were dispatched to bombard the strong-points ashore, they had none of the effect that they had caused at Salerno. Even the hundreds of Fortresses which flew over us several days in succession to drop bombs did not have visible immediate result, though I could not see how the enemy troops could live through the tremendous pounding which they received.

From a purely personal angle our difficulties were increasing: we had a series of discouraging signals from the shore about our gun-fire; apparently unexploded shells were falling over the town, harbour and shipping; our arc of fire was accordingly restricted and there seemed very few opportunities for firing. Stores were running short, although our old enemy *Bangkok* turned up and could not have been more generous. My Flotilla Officer was sympathetic but ineffectual in his efforts to get our release from the area. Finally I persuaded him to go ashore and have a look round; he did, and came back with sailing instructions for one of the Flak ships retained in the follow-up to the operation.

There were three of us left: 16, 14 (commanded by my old 4th Flotilla comrade Bill Bailey) and another who had had the worst time hitherto of any of us. She had had casualties at Dieppe and an appalling time at Vibo Valentia during the early Italian days, where she had given a very fine display of gallantry. It had been a minor landing for LCTs and the Flak was sent to support them; there had been unexpected resistance, and she had told the Ts not to beach until she had settled the hash of an enemy emplacement which was endangering the venture. She stationed herself off the shore and engaged it at point-blank range, which was not part of the commitments of an ack-ack ship. She had succeeded, however, though her crew had paid toll. At Anzio she had been in the noisiest sector, and the nerves of some members of the ship's company had suffered. She was commanded by an intrepid young officer of extraordinary stamina and guts, who died in 1953 after years of ill health brought on by the strain.

It was patently obvious which ship should be released, and we gave way willingly. Bill B. honestly preferred to be in the thick of things, and the morale of his crew was at a new high due to a similar success to ours with an enemy aircraft, also confirmed by the Admiralty. So we stayed on, and Bill gave us tea and moral support as we lay for days a few hundred yards from the harbour entrance. We needed both badly, as we were all starting to get a bit nervy with the ceaseless closing-up of guns and shelling from unseen directions. The Germans were making a series of counter-attacks, and Hitler had issued orders through Kesselring that at all costs the raiders must be driven back into the sea. On the other hand the Ts kept bumbling on in and out of the harbour with superb aplomb, but they did see a bit of life and have a change of company every day. I know we were getting sick of the sight of each other in the wardroom, and only Knotty remained calm and collected as he perused old copies of the *Field*. I started to play Patience desperately with frightful bets with myself on the result. 'If it doesn't come out this time,' I would say sharply, 'the ship will be blown up to-morrow.' Or, 'If it comes out, we shall be released in three days.' This latter meant going on playing for hours and hours. But finally we got our sailing orders, and one evening in February we beetled off in the middle of an alarm. All passages to Naples were made at night, as the coast between Anzio and Gela was enemy held, and with fruity shooting, great fun could be had by all except the ship concerned. The channel was mined at night, but it was a risk I was quite prepared for, and I heaved a sigh of relief as we passed through the Ischia Channel. I turned over to Trevor at this point and told him to take the machine back to Naples and wake me outside the harbour entrance. We were senior ship and Flak 14 followed us meekly. I was woken after a splendid snooze, and came up on the bridge in time to salute the *Hambledon*, our Salerno Destroyer friend, whose officers waved frantically at us. I felt pretty heroic until Priest handed me three signals which he had received from the authorities. They all read roughly the same: 'Give reasons in writing why you have just crossed two minefields.'

They were from FOIC (Flag-Officer in Charge). One seemed angrier than the others and told me to report in person. I studied my sailing orders, which read with crystal clarity: 'From the bottom of the Ischia Channel proceed to Naples.' I asked Trevor if he had done anything quaint and he denied it. After I had berthed I rushed over to Bill Bailey.

'Did you know that I had taken you over a minefield or two?' I asked.

'Of course,' said this surprising individual. 'Haven't you read CSX No. 1631?'

I had certainly not seen CSX 1631 (a secret navigational message), having only been issued with numbers up to 953.

'Why the bloody hell didn't you call me up?' I said to Bill.

He replied that as I had the FO on board, he presumed that I was acting under special instructions. The FO, armed with my sailing signals, got me out of this dilemma, and I only received a mild reprimand.

Naples seemed like paradise after Anzio, and I found a lot of old chums in and around the port. Pat Brown and Jimmy Parrish were there with Public Relations, and Tony Beckwith turned up as a BBC correspondent. Another amusing person was Hugh Barty-King, an ex-schoolmate and then working for the 8th Army newspaper, the *Union Jack*. The latter invited me to some bewildering parties, where famous Neapolitan opera singers beat the hell out of *Rose Marie* in order to please the English. Naples was now in full swing as a leave and entertainment centre. It was an ideal place for the serviceman, as anything could be bought for food or cigarettes. There were masses of canteens and trips to all the interesting and historical sights of the neighbourhood. The crew enjoyed a trip to Pompeii, but seemed to remember the drawings on the wall more vividly than the other items. I had suddenly lost my desire to 'see things', and was content to entertain my friends on board or go to one of the officers' clubs. There was a small orchestra at the main one of these, where an Italian songstress warbled 'Lili Marlene' and 'Chiribiribin' with a voice which blew the soup off the plates. It was a current story that she and the band had not stopped operating for any evening during the switch-over from German to British audiences, and she now created fresh havoc in the hearts of susceptible officers. In fact, she could have carried a sash with 'We never closed' written on it with impunity.

It was difficult to believe, amidst all this rather phoney gaiety, that less than a hundred miles away two different battles for dear life were in progress, and I felt that our rest could not go on indefinitely. We had about a week in port and then the FO came to the ship and told me to prepare to go up to Anzio again. When I found that we were to go alone I was indignant. Although the two Flaks who had been with us there recently were genuinely defective, I could not see why one of the four others, wintering in either Messina or Bari, should not have a basinful. Quite frankly I dreaded our return to the beach-head, and I knew that the crew would feel hard done by. The ship we had replaced in the first place was fit and available, and anyhow, there seemed no justification for our presence now that the coastal batteries were established. The FO promised to signal for a relief, but we had to go. I stored ship, stuffed the wardroom with camellias, and told the crew what they were in for frankly, but expressing complete confidence in their support. I did, however, make a grave tactical error. Having been assured by both the FO and the base that a relief would arrive within five days, I mentioned this limit on our stay, a step I was to regret, particularly on the thirteenth day of our forthcoming visit. Ts returning in the past few days to Naples had warned us that conditions at Anzio had deteriorated, and

I was surprised on our arrival to find at first sight no appreciable change. The Ts were still chugging away and there were plenty of Liberty Ships to unload. It was not until I anchored close to the harbour entrance and had a good look through the binoculars that I could see the difference. The buildings near the harbour were mostly in ruins and the jetties had ominous breaks and cracks in them. As I let go the anchor, a shell landed just by our starboard quarter and I realized that 'Annie' did definitely live here still. An LCA[5] came out to the ship with instructions to take me ashore to meet the CO of the shore batteries, who was American. I told Trevor that if the shelling got intensive he was to move the machine, and toddled off ashore.

The scene in the harbour was wonderfully calm. Negro stevedores were unloading with great cheerfulness and rapidity. I was met by one of the base landing-craft officers, who told me some of the details of the battle which was raging. Heroism seemed common-place, and for once all the Services and the two Allies were working as one. The quantity alone of the stuff unloaded had made Anzio the third largest port in the world in this respect, and as it was about the size of Mevagissey, the work involved was staggering. The shelling was now almost continuous and sleep was only possible in underground shelters. The naval base with a skeleton staff was magnificently keeping its head, and no praise can be high enough for the LCTs. Some of them had had over fifty days of this nightmarish existence and how they managed to carry on was a mystery. Apart from the bi-weekly appearance of the LCT which brought Naafi stores, there was no consolation, and they had to rely solely on comradeship and stamina.

I picked my way through the rubble and finally tracked down the American with whom I had an appointment. He was a Colonel of depressingly jovial aspect, and I had an alarming interview.

'Say, you've got one of those Flak ships, haven't you?' he started off, and I nodded apprehensively.

'Waal, I guess we can use you in our barrage scheme every night. I

[5] Landing Craft Assault

think I'll run a telephone out to you so that we can keep in the closest touch.'

I was shaken by the prospect, and told him that owing to our insecure anchor facilities we might drag in bad weather and take the telephone with us. I did not dare to tell him that we would also drag it with us when shelling got too accurate. It was also unlikely that he would get his phone back, even if he did press Button B.

He was clearly discouraged, and asked if the ship was visible. I gaily replied that she lay outside the harbour entrance and tried to find her with his binoculars. I hastily put them down, as I could see HMLCF 16 careering out to sea at a rate of knots.

'And very wise too,' I said to myself.

On the other hand, I told the bewildered Colonel that I had instructed the First Lieutenant to carry out speed trials. He could not have believed such an improbable story, but after a quick look at my ship said:

'Jesus, is that a Flak ship? It looks more like a barge to me.'

We had reached an impasse, and gathering up what remained of my dignity I made my way back to the harbour. Unpleasant as things were aboard, they were doubly so ashore, I mused, as I fastened my tin hat farther on my head and broke into a swift trot.

After chasing my ship out to sea I boarded her and discovered that several near misses had caused Trevor quite justifiably to increase the range. But a definite lull took me back to within 500 yards of the port, a position which we were to maintain almost continuously for the worst fortnight in my life, although I suppose it is too soon to come to that conclusion. We were to be closed up for twenty hours out of the twenty-four, and were hardly ever in a position to warrant opening fire; we were to come into close contact with the whole bag of the enemy's more ingenious tricks, and our nerves were to be stretched to twanging point. There were the rocket bombs, and although they were aimed at bigger game (a brand-new battleship was an early success), there was something terrifying about the way they turned and twisted in their flight. There were the midget submarines which crept up in the night, and E-boats perpetually on the war-path. But worst of all were the acoustic mines which low-flying aircraft used to drop in the area at dusk. These only went off when a number of ships had already gone safely over them; they tried to drop them in the main channel, but there were numerous outlying bosh-shots. The channel itself was swept every morning before the LSTs and LCTs were permitted into the harbour, but where we were stationed was either not swept at all or swept later in the day. I had a feverish time trying to choose between taking the anchor up and going to a swept area, or staying put and hoping that as we swung round with the tide we would not touch them off. We saw two go up within a hundred yards, and both contacting craft had astonishing escapes with their crews. The first was an RAF rescue launch which was going at top speed and got past before the mine exploded. The other was a DUKW[6] which got away with only its stern blown off. We watched the two incidents with awe in our gaze, but had the common sense to lower the dinghy for the fish which littered the scenes of the explosions.

Our only activity was taking part in the big smokescreen laying which took place every dusk. We luckily had hundreds of smoke floats and it seemed to justify our existence in a minor way. Apart from this we watched hopefully for our relief ship to arrive, and most of the crew thought out what they would say to other Flaks of our acquaintance if and when we returned. One of the crew got ill with severe jaundice and we had to transfer him to a hospital ship. Against every rule of international warfare these mercy craft came quite unarmed to within a few hundred yards of the harbour entrance. I could only surmise that so dire was the need to get stores and ammunition ashore that small ships simply could not be spared to take the wounded out. I know that I used to stand with bated breath while the hospital ships were in the vicinity, and it was a great relief when they sailed back.

It took very little to stir and excite us these days, and there were happenings of splendour to pierce the gloom. There was, for instance, the sight of hundreds of Fortresses going over to try to break the enemy bloc. The cheers that went up from the shore could

---

[6] Amphibious Craft. Their name was derived from the factory serial letters of the firm which produced them.

be heard on board and vice versa. One incident is embedded for ever in my mind, because we were almost the closest eyewitnesses: a Flying Fortress got hit before she could deliver her load, and in order not to drop over the town, she made out to sea. She landed near us, and the Captain's timing and nerve were so impeccable that she stayed afloat long enough for the entire crew to emerge unscathed before she sank.

Then there was the Bill Duthie affair. I was trying to get thirty-nine winks in my cabin when I was shaken by a violent crash: Trevor came down and said it was my old skipper. Bill appeared, looking drawn and haggard, and asked me if I wanted any food. He had understood that we had difficulty in getting stores and he had a heavy load. I was touched by the gesture and gratefully accepted. Trevor went and organized the transfer, and Bill and I dipped deep into the gin bottle. A Red Warning was issued and I said good-bye to him at the top of the hatch.

'Tell me, Bill. Was I the worst Number One you've ever had?' I asked.

His eyes filled with tears.

'Easily,' he replied, and I never saw him again. The following day he was killed in the harbour and his Number One (Jackie Holmes, who saw two COs die in succession while he was on board) took over. My crew were getting restive, and with only three officers to share the watches the position was becoming steadily worse. I signalled to the FO for a relief and got no satisfaction except an infuriating letter which read: 'I should stay quietly where you are until a replacement can be found.' By the same post I received a memorandum from the Squadron Commander about morale and the safeguarding of same. The inferences which had caused its issue were obvious, but it was not very tactful in its time of arrival. Written by a man who had spent one comparatively pleasant day at Anzio, it was a vitriolic and unnecessary document which made me blind with rage. I penned several pages in reply. As the sole representative of his Squadron at present at Anzio, I was able to tell him something of the conditions, so that a more generous view could be taken in Messina, some thousand miles away from the front line.

I took to the bottle in desperation, but I do not think it affected me either for better or worse. I stayed on the bridge permanently and made terrible jokes into the microphone. On the radio from the Port Wave station would come the information that eighty Junkers were approaching the harbour. 'Oh,' I would mutter into the mike, 'I can only see seventy-nine.' Or 'I think that's a Handley Page,' as the latest type of enemy aircraft sped by, dropping *billet-doux* as she went. I hope never to recapture the fears that passed through my mind during these crucial days. I like to think now that the fear of giving way in front of the lads overruled my personal terror. But the sheer physical fatigue caused by constant watchfulness was almost insufferable. I am told that there were innumerable cases of desertion from duty both ashore and afloat during this operation, but the medical authorities said that the circumstances were exceptional when direst penalties were threatened. I know I was several times within an ace of complete breakdown, but I was saved by two things: the faith that the boys expressed in their faces and the fantastic example set by the LCTs. On the thirteenth morning LCF 10 (our salvagee from Salerno) hove in sight, and she must have been staggered by the warmth of her reception. I cruelly broke the facts of life to her and practically waltzed the ship into the channel home. Our relief sent us a signal as we departed, about her relief, and I made a mental note that under no circumstances would it be us.

The Bay of Naples seemed heavenly to us as we closed the harbour on our return journey. I even forgot to cross my usual minefield. But as soon as we berthed I got ready some of the speeches I had prepared for the authorities. I considered that I had been badly let down and I wanted to know the reason for it. When the FO walked on board with a present of oranges, Trevor walked straight out of the wardroom and Knotty went on deck. Choking with rage I let fly; I may have been a bit hysterical, for the news of Bill's death was broken to me now, and I could not restrain my feelings. All the pent-up emotion burst, and the unfortunate Flotilla Officer got it hot and strong. I do not know how the interview ended, but a copy of a signal from him to Messina was handed to me in the afternoon. It read: 'LCF 16 returned from Anzio in critical condition. Request immediate relief.' I was absolutely furious at this new development, for the message could only be interpreted in one way, and that would cause another Memorandum on Morale, besides casting a stigma on the ship. I rushed ashore, and fortunately caught Lieut-Commander Richey, at that time Senior Officer of Landing Craft in Naples. I hurriedly explained the position, and he sent a cancellation of the signal on his own initiative. He soothed me down and took me to lunch. The FO, bewildered by my recovery and at a loss to know my real feelings, tried to make amends in his own peculiar fashion by writing to the Squadron Commander and repeating the letter to everyone in the Mediterranean, quoting us as the supreme example of gallantry in action. This bizarre overstatement annoyed me almost as much as his first signal. All I wanted, I told him, was to remove any suggestion of loss of morale from my ship's company. Why, we were perfectly willing and able to go up to Anzio again if we were needed: a boast which I was to regret bitterly when we were given sailing orders for the God-forsaken port a week later.

But for the moment I was blissfully unaware of my foolishness and revelled in my return to normality. I slept, fed and was very happy indeed. Leslie Henson was visiting Naples with his 'Gaieties', a show which featured several old theatrical friends, and Dave Hutcheson inveigled Leslie aboard 16. It was a wonderful thing for us all, as the great comedian entertained the ship's company in the mess-deck for nearly an hour. He was in terrific form, and as the last ship he had played in had been the *King George V*, it was a great compliment that he paid us. The lads' letters were full of him when they wrote home, and one went so far as to say, 'It's almost worth while putting up with the skipper if he can get people like Leslie Henson aboard.' I took him back that evening to the theatre and sat in the wings watching the show in an emotional state of mind because I had just got my sailing orders for Anzio. Watching Hermione Baddeley being excruciatingly funny and Walter Crisham dancing gracefully with Prudence Hyman seemed the most heart-breaking thing in the world and I could not help wondering when I would be free to sit in a stall in a London theatre again. The Flotilla Officer had cautiously vanished before I could contact him about our return to the battle area, and it appeared that he had gone to Messina to try to fetch a relief.

We took over from LCF 10, who seemed as relieved at our advent as we had been at hers ten days before. We were in for a gruelling time, it was obvious, and on this occasion I gave the crew no probable length of stay. It turned out to be the least wearing period, as the weather was so bad that unloading was suspended half the time and the enemy did not waste so many shells. The Ts were still at it, some in a half-sinking condition, some with slightly bibulous captains and crews, but all behaving with incredible resilience and tenacity. I got sick of cruising around and dropped my anchor, letting out every inch of wire cable I possessed. The seas were big and came right over the ship from time to time, and food had to be handed up through the engine-room hatch, as the quarterdeck was permanently awash. Our static position was a source of wonder to all beholders, including ourselves, and I can only imagine that the anchor was as tired as we were and could not be bothered to drag. This time we were relieved by LCF 15, and we were so deep in a coma that we did not even send her a witty signal. As I sailed away for what was really our final exit from the not so old-world or picturesque little town of Anzio, I reflected that we had outlasted in endurance any ship of our complement, and that nothing could make me forget the unity and the strength of the loyalty which officers and men of HMLCF 16 had given me during the whole of this critical era.

PART THREE

Screen, Stage and Typewriter

5
I Have My Chance (and Miss It)

There is a famous theatrical anecdote related of the late Lilian Baylis and a wretched actor who was sent on at a moment's notice to play Hamlet (full-length version) at the Old Vic. Having stumbled through the role, and on his knees with gratitude at having got through it all, he fell sweating into the arms of Miss Baylis, who was waiting for him to come off the stage. 'Well, you've 'ad your chance,' she said grimly, 'and missed it.'

I feel rather the same about an unfortunate excursion of mine into the realms of the Bioscope in the summer of 1947 and onwards. I had had a bad year and was anxious to lay my hands on anything that brought in the doubloons. I was suddenly summoned to Ealing Film Studios for a small part in a film about to be shot there dealing with the Affaire Koenigsmark. Thither I hied, and was making my way to the casting office when I ran into Mr Basil Dearden who was to direct the film. He remarked that he did not know I was out of the navy, let alone hoping to be in his film. But suddenly a strange look came into his face and he told me not to leave the building until I had seen him again.

So I carried on with my normal business and saw the casting director, Roger Ould, who was courteous and kind until interrupted by a phone call, during which he stared at me as if I was a Thing from Outer Space. I wondered if I'd got leprosy or some obscure plague, but he put the instrument down and announced that the director and producer of the film wished to see me. I was ushered into the art department (the producer, Michael Relph, also designed the miraculous sets and costumes), and after a brief exchange of pleasantries, Mr Relph looked me over, hummed and hahed, and told me that that very afternoon one of the leading parts in their projected film had become, as they say in the columns of the *Stage*, unexpectedly vacant. Was I prepared to make a test for the role?

Was I not!!!!

The character was George-Louis of Hanover (subsequently George I of England), the film was entitled *Saraband for Dead Lovers*, after the book by Helen Simpson, and the other leading parts were to be played by Stewart Granger, Françoise Rosay, Flora Robson, Frederick Valk and Joan Greenwood. It was to be made in Technicolor and was to take several months.

I travelled back in the tube from Ealing suspended on air, and reported a few days later and made an elaborate test, dressed largely in Dennis Price's boots and something as usual that had been worn by Robert Morley. At the end of a gruelling day Mr Dearden, who had been kindness and patience themselves, informed me that the part was as good as mine and that I'd be hearing from them in a few days after everyone concerned had viewed the test. I waited for two weeks and, unable to contain myself in London, asked for permission to leave for Cornwall. They said it was all right, but that I must be prepared to return at a moment's notice. I left for the West Country, happily unaware that they were stuffing the faces of all the character actors in town, testing them in the hope that they could (as one says in poker) 'improve'. After I had landed the part, I met at least half a dozen actors who had expected to get it.

So there I was, down at Mevagissey, trying and indeed succeeding to forget the whole business while I stayed with one of my ex-shipmates, Ken Shearwood. After a year of strenuous fishing with the local fleet, he was running a curiously irregular tripper-ship service to neighbouring seaside resorts, and I was roped in mainly to collect the fares, which he disliked doing, and to keep the customers occupied while he fiddled with the engines of the fairly good ship *Coral*. As there were no lifeboats supplied and his mechanical knowledge was practically *nil*, I had to do some pretty strenuous overacting in order that alarm and despondency didn't spread.

I had almost given up hope of ever appearing in any entertainment again, let alone in glorious Technicolor, when suddenly a telegram arrived from the Ealing casting director which read: *'Congratulations – you have the part. Can you write?* OULD.' I sent back a telegram, saying, *'Thanks ever so. Yes.'* And it wasn't until several weeks later that I learnt to my cost that what he meant was 'Can you ride?'

Anyhow, I beetled back to London, and apart from throwing the make-up department into a frenzy by being as black as a berry, everyone was delightful and appeared to be delighted that I had been assigned the role. I was to get thirty pounds a day, which seemed excessive, but all my friends as usual said I should have asked for fifty. The location shots were to be done at Woodstock, outside and around Blenheim Palace. Accommodation had been booked at the Bear Hotel, and thither I repaired. It was still high summer, and one of those rare lovely ones at that. I had read the script, realized that I had the best part in the film, and was sick with terror. However, after meeting Joan Greenwood, with whom I had at least half my scenes, I was greatly reassured. A sweeter, funnier, more disarming lady you could not meet, and I was soon potty about her. Jill Balcon, another charmer, was playing her lady-in-waiting, and the three of us became inseparable.

My dad was played by the late Frederick Valk, who was expecting his first child at the time. He was in consequence fairly restless, and I used to go for long walks with him in the evenings. He was an enormous great dear, who loved England and the English and had indeed bought the *Encyclopaedia Britannica* on the instalment plan, and was working his way quietly through it. One night, for some unknown reason, we were discussing public schools, whose system is or was my pet hate. Freddie asked me where I had been educated.

'Winchester,' I replied.

'Vinchester?' he said. 'You remember Diana Qvirk?'

'Oh yes, indeed,' I replied. 'We used to whistle at her in chapel.'

He let out a gargantuan laugh.

'I married Diana Qvirk', he said.

I got to know the Valk family very well, and enchanting they were. His sudden death robbed the stage of a fine actor and his children of a most delightful papa. He was very kind to me, and helped me with my German for the captain in *The African Queen*, a role he should actually have played.

Mr Granger had not arrived, and owing to the alarming reports we had heard of his behaviour and language, we were a bit worried. However, Michael Gough, who was surprisingly playing my brother, said he'd just been in a film with Mr Granger, and that he was a dear. It seemed an unlikely description, and we waited anxiously. The 'dear' arrived, with the largest car one had ever seen, a caravan dressing-room in tow, and a very smart chauffeur carrying a lot of cases of champagne. These were produced at dinner the same night, and we all had a fairly uncosy meal. Afterwards, the Misses Greenwood, Balcon and I sat in a little sitting-room discussing the visitor, when he entered, asked for tea for four, and in a few minutes had become a very ordinary and delightful person. We sat up until four, and ended the evening drinking, as far as I can remember, lemon squash and Eno's, a drink to which I'm particularly addicted in hot weather.

Throughout the film he was fantastically kind to me. He must have known my part was a very good one indeed, but he helped me, gave me sound advice and started a friendship that has endured throughout the years. I can see he can make an appalling impression on some people, as he is fiercely intolerant and impatient of inefficiency and phoniness. But to most actors, his behaviour is impeccable, and his generosity to those having a bad time is legendary. It is only when he comes up against two-faced stars, two-headed directors, and inquisitive press gentlemen, that the storm breaks and heaven help anyone within spitting distance. He'll be horrified when he reads this, as I think he secretly likes to be thought an Ogre, about whom years after his demise someone will write something nice.

So there we were at Woodstock, embarking on a film which was to be the crowning achievement of the British cinema. Indeed, a book on the actual shooting of the film was already being planned, and little did they think at this time that they would eventually have to beg Mr Granger to sign a great many copies in order to sell some of the surplus.

My opening scene was unfortunately to be on a horse. I had by this time cleared up the 'writing-riding' misunderstanding, and was taking a few lessons from some patient lady equestrian. I came to a sort of understanding with an animal called Peter, but only after some very nasty moments indeed. There was one day when Peter could only be said to be running away with Peter, and I was trying to think how to stop him, when a gentleman in country costume said, 'Where do you think you are going, might I ask?' 'Oh, I wish I knew,' I replied sadly, as I whizzed past him, realizing in my flight that it was the Duke of Marlborough in person.

The day came for the first shot. My mistress (in the film), Frau Busche, and I were on our horses, and fortunately it was (they thought) to be a static shot. I say fortunately, because dear Megs Jenkins, who was playing Mrs Busche, dreaded horses, and had made it quite clear, even in her contract, that her horse was not to move. It was really quite a simple scene, although about eight people were required to keep the horses in position, including, now I come to think of it, the director Basil Dearden, who 'knew all about horses'. But what made me a bit windy was that Peter had been sacked from carrying me, and his successor was a bit haughty, although they assured me that he was more photogenic than Peter, a statement that bored the pants off me. When it came to my turn to throw a purse at a non-existent beggar lady or gent I aimed inaccurately, and hit the snitch of Frau Busche's animal, who was not unnaturally livid and reared up in rage. Miss Jenkins nearly had a fit, and it was several hours before horses, actors and directors made any sense at all.

It wasn't a happy day and I offered my resignation, which I tend to do on the first day of any acting enterprise, because I can always say later on, 'Yah boo, I told you so.' Basil ignored this, and I suggested that I'd better get to know my new horse, and off I slunk into the woods where it refused to move or even say 'Neigh'.

The next day was worse. We were all posted to a small hill in the grounds of Blenheim. I had everything on, including the kitchen stove, wigs, hats, swords, daggers and a Roussel Belt.

'On the word "Action",' said Basil Dearden calmly, 'I want you to ride as quickly as possible over to that coach where Freddie Valk is standing.'

I looked into the far distance where I could see a tiny figure beside a vehicle.

'As quickly as possible?' I asked.

'Yes,' said Basil grimly.

'Action' came, and I stuck my foot or heel into the flanks of the horse. It ambled quietly down the slope, and came to a dead stop by some rather nice grass, where it proceeded to have its tea break. We had three like this, and every time the beast stopped at the same place. Basil was in despair.

'We'd better use the riding double,' he said coldly.

For some unknown reason I got puce with rage, and demanded another 'take'.

'Give the horse a great bash,' I shouted at its owner, standing by.

Basil yelled 'Action', its owner clouted it, and I went off at about a hundred and ten mph. The hat, wig and sword flew off in the first fifty yards, and almost my Roussel Belt, but the horse continued as if possessed, and drew up at its original spot, dead if you know what I mean.

I picked up my wig, my hat, and my sword, and, with as much dignity as I could muster, wandered back. I didn't speak to Basil, but handed him my wig, my hat, my sword and my theoretical notice. I sulked off to a deckchair to get comforted by Miss Flora Robson. I watched the riding double don my hat, my wig and my sword, and mount the beast. Very professionally he rode off on 'Action', and even more professionally the horse stopped at its usual spot. I was beginning to feel very sorry for Freddie Valk, so near and yet so far, and waiting for a horseman who never seemed able to make it. The riding double came back, and Basil, by then almost apoplectic, ordered the owner of the horse into the saddle. He was as thin as a rake, but nonetheless donned my hat, my wig, my sword, but not my Roussel Belt. For the umpteenth time, Basil shouted 'Action'.

I slumped back in my chair.

'Please, God,' I whispered, 'let that dear horse stop where it always does.'

I closed my eyes with this blasphemy, and opened them to see Basil dancing about with fury. My prayers had been answered, and that's why, dear filmgoer, you never saw George-Louis of Hanover greet his father in the forest of Celle.

After that, I was kept strictly off a horse, but we went into Oxford to view what are unaccountably called the 'the rushes', [1] and the scene where I threw the purse at Frau Horse's busche (I mean Frau Busche's horse) showed us upside down, which is the sort of thing that can only happen to actors like me.

Back at Ealing, everything went smoothly until they asked me to have all my hair cut off. I wasn't v. keen, although they said that it would make my hair grow stronger than ever before, but they experimented with rubber wigs, and finally decided that it would have to be done. Like the great fool that I am, I didn't hold my locks to ransom or I could have paid for some of the treatment I have given my head since that catastrophic day. Mark you, as my mother would say, they did it in the nicest possible way; I did a scene in the morning with all my hair on, and then a Mr Taylor, who has since left for South Africa, shaved my hair to within a quarter of an inch or less, and Wham! there was I, plunged into a terrifying sadistic scene with my wife (Miss Greenwood). I now know exactly how the French collaborators felt when they got their deserts, and speaking for myself, I shall never collaborate again. It's torture on the pillow at night, and I finally had to wear one of those little woolly caps which the Arabs wear to show that they have been circumcised, which is that sort of thing anyhow. But I did at least find out who were my true friends. They were the ones who didn't visibly blench when walking with me through the streets. I did really look like something out of a space-fiction book, and the villagers at the place where Mr Granger had his country residence started a rumour that I was his dotty brother who was kept under lock and key in the attic.

It was singularly unattractive, and I was at low resistance ebb, when I had to start beating the daylights out of my beloved Miss Greenwood. Basil Dearden kept us a great many days on this scene,

[1] Results of the previous day's shooting

and it was I who usually ended up crying because blood started trickling out of Miss G's mouth. When you want not to hurt someone, you generally end by doing them mortal injury, and I couldn't bear these scenes, even if the script dictated so. I forgot to explain that I had to be completely bald, in order that the audience would be sufficiently shocked when I took my wig off, before entering the bridal chamber on my wedding night. Shocked they were, and, on the general release, a pretty good giggle was had by north of the river cinema addicts one week, and by south of the river *ditto* the next. Twice I had to be re-shaved before the end of the film, because of an irritating thing called 'continuity', and as for 'growing stronger', that's the silliest thing I've ever heard. I spent a vast fortune with some ladies in Sloane Street who paint your pate with iodine, which makes you look as if you've been scalped, some sadists in New York, who pour boiling oil on your head, and vibrate it until you are dizzy, to say nothing of sulphur shampoos, magnetic combs, standing on my head, lying at an incline, and other pursuits, in an attempt to bring back my pre-*Saraband* hair.

But still none of that would have mattered if I'd become a star overnight, and stolen a march on Mr Yul Brynner. The film came out, and I went to the gala-gala première with Mr Granger, and the press hated it, the public couldn't understand it, and hundreds of thousands of pounds went down the drain. But they adored it in Yugoslavia, Japan, and I believe Minorca, and I owe my only steady fan to the film. He is a sex maniac, and lives in Cologne. I say sex maniac, because I cannot imagine an ordinary fan asking for a picture of me wrestling naked. But that is what he did. 'I have seen *Saraband* thrice,' he wrote, 'and may I say you are delicious in your burliness. To me you are far more handsome than such as Stewart Granger.'

Here followed a request for a photo. Funnily enough, I have no pictures handy of me wrestling naked, but my friends, including Mr Granger, on reading this extraordinary letter, insisted on my replying to it, a step which I was to regret.

'Dear Herr W,' I wrote. 'Thank you for your nice unusual letter. I'm afraid I have no pictures of me wrestling naked, but perhaps this will do.' I enclosed a wartime snap of myself on a camel near the Sphinx, which I regret to say sent my fan delirious with joy.

'My dearest Peter Bull,' he wrote. 'I cannot tell you what pleasure you with the camel give me. I love you, Peter Bull, and would like to be your big chum. Have you by chance also a picture of your full corporation in bathing drawers?'

This froze me into silence, but he still writes occasionally, and I have a horror that he will suddenly turn up in Chelsea and frighten the daylights out of my daily.

Basil Dearden was not unnaturally deeply depressed by the public reaction to *Saraband for Dead Lovers*, but he seems to bear me no grudge and even employs me from time to time, although I must admit it is in some role which requires humiliation or violence to be dished out to the character. I am very fond of him indeed and I like it when he rings up as he did the other year and said: 'Will you be blown up to-morrow, Peter?' 'Yes, of course, Basil,' I replied meekly.

So the next day I reported for a film, dressed up to the nines in a Dictator's uniform and was made to kick off at a foreign football match. The whole point of the scene was that the ball, heavily mined, should explode in my face and blow me to smithereens. I do not know if any of you have ever tried running to kick a football and then stopping dead just as your toes connect, but that is what I had to do, so that the shot could be 'tricked'; and very difficult it was, I don't mind telling you. It was quite a funny day's work, though I never asked the name of the film, got paid fifty smackers for a morning's work and tootled happily off home.

The next one Mr Dearden engaged me for was even more degrading but a good deal more lucrative. In this film I had to be drenched to the skin, have a pie thrown at my face ('What's the fellow aiming at?' was the cue), have the pie frozen on to my face (chipped off with a chisel by Nick Phipps) and end with some icicles hanging on the end of my nose. It wasn't a frightfully attractive part and it was for a comedy called *Who Done It?* I imagine the next offer to come from Mr D. will be one of those lifeboat numbers, where one spends days and nights getting in and out of the water while the tank, in which the film is being shot, gets smellier and smellier.

I had enough of that in *The African Queen*. Though I was and still am very proud of being in that (to me) superb film, there was one quite horrid day swimming about in a tank which hadn't been emptied for months. I have to admit that Miss Katharine Hepburn was in a boat dishing out the brandy, which made a big difference, but the taste of the water is with me still.

Being chosen to play the German Captain in this film was one of the most exciting things that has happened to me, and I was really desperate to land the job. It all came up very suddenly while I was at the Alexandra Palace, about to embark on the second transmission of a TV play called *The Silent Inn*. It was in this that I enacted the part of the heavyweight champion of the world, although it was written for the lightweight one. We had finished a heavyweight lunch and I was summoned to the phone by my agent just as we were about to embark on a final run-through.

'If you want to play a goodish part in *The African Queen*,' he announced, 'you have got to be at Isleworth Studios by six.'

It was, as you can imagine, not a very convenient appointment, and to get to Isleworth from Muswell Hill is not exactly child's play. You are also forbidden by contract to leave the area when about to transmit, but on the pretence of visiting a not very probable sick friend in hospital at Wood Green, I escaped in a car about five, without more than a shilling on me, met John Huston, the director of the film, spoke a few words of German for the part, clinched the deal and whirled back to the Ally-Pally, cashed a cheque, paid the chauffeur and went through the TV in a daze.

The trouble, I thought, with the final scenes of *The African Queen* was that the film went to pieces with the arrival of the German Captain, though for once it was not entirely my fault. After the miraculous long scenes in which Miss Hepburn and Mr Bogart were the sole protagonists, the slightly phoney happy ending was bound to jar. But non-professionally it was a happy time, and I was knocked sideways by the stars' integrity and kindness. On the first day at the studios Miss Hepburn, to whom I had not even been introduced, insisted on the third star dressing-room, which had been empty since Robert Morley's departure, being allotted to me. I had many lunches with her and the Bogart family, and though they teased me a bit about an unfortunate film called *Salute the Toff* in which I was also engaged at the time, I adored being with them.

I did not see the film till some time after it had opened, but I got rather irritated by the number of viewers who asked me if I had used my own voice in the film. It was then that I discovered that indeed my voice had been par-dubbed by Walter Rilla and jolly cleverly at that.

6
The Lady's Not for Burning

Why does one (or perhaps I should say, do I) remember disasters so much more vividly than successes? Certainly, in stage biographies, the Success Story in the theatre is now so hackneyed that the reader must instinctively long for a taste of mishap. To judge from some books of this sort, even if the show has had a short run, it is made abundantly clear that the author or authoress made a great 'personal success', whatever that may mean. But let it not be thought that I have never appeared in a success, and I suppose the most distinguished one was *The Lady's Not for Burning*. This production was not only to prove epoch-making in the history of the theatre, but more important still (for me) was to establish a lot of friendships in the company which have lasted to the present day.

It all started when morale, to say nothing of bank balance, was very much in the red, and I had not been allowed to display myself on a stage since the war. A lady I knew, principally as an actress, called Marjorie Stewart, was casting director at the Arts Theatre, at this time administered by Alec Clunes. She sent me a script of the Christopher Fry play, of which I understood about an eighth at first reading, but it was impossible to ignore the beautiful writing and above all the excruciatingly funny jokes dotted through the piece. I was pretty entranced by my part, which only started in the second act but was full of lovely things.

The play was written in verse, but although this fact made the project more intimidating, I could never view it as such, and once I had got used to the language, it seemed no different from ordinary dialogue. The first reading was highly successful, and we all had the feeling we were embarking on something of exceptional quality. Jack Hawkins was directing, and Alec Clunes was to play the leading male part, Thomas Mendip, a gent who threw a whole village into turmoil by wanting to be and indeed insisting on being hanged. The part of Jennet Jourdemayne, the girl accused of witchcraft, had been written for Pamela Brown. Owing to her non-availability at this time Sheila Manahan, straight from her great success in *Happy as Larry*, was entrusted with it. The two brothers were played by Michael Gough and Gordon Whiting, the young clerk by Derek Blomfield and his adored one by Daphne Slater. Henzie Raeburn was the Mayor's wife, and the character men were acted by Andrew Leigh (Mayor), Frank Napier (Chaplain) and Morris Sweden, who was to prove wildly funny as the rag-and-bone man, Skipps.

It was only scheduled to run two and a half weeks at the Arts Theatre, as there were previous commitments for the theatre and some of the actors. Financially it was bound to be a wash-out, but somehow the prospect did not worry me. Christopher Fry came to all the rehearsals, and his quiet dry wit and enchanting modesty made the rehearsals gay and relaxed, and the only fly in the ointment was Jack Hawkins breaking his leg during this period and having to direct in agony and plaster.

The play went very well on the first night, 10 March 1948, but the notices were mixed. Some critics opined that the meaning was obscure and difficult to follow, but most of them had the good sense to realize that it was a new type of verse play. There was, however, no doubt about its popular appeal to the patrons of the arts or indeed the Arts, and we were packed for the short run. One's actor friends raved about it, and Miss Hermione Gingold came both Sundays. The dressing-rooms on the Sunday nights were thronged with stars, and it was quite droll one night, when the rafters had rung with praise and all the usual vociferous utterances of fellow actors saying 'darlings, darlings, it was wonderful, marvellous, divine', when an old school friend of mine tapped at the door and said, 'Thought I'd come and see you to tell you that I've had a most interesting evening and this is John Abercrombie who didn't like it at all,' and a rather sad bespectacled gent was ushered into the room to face a lot of rather hysterical artistes.

We were all desperately sad when the run finished, and I suppose the general feeling was that *The Lady's Not for Burning* would not be heard of again. For no one seemed anxious to buy the play for the commercial theatre, and had it not been for an energetic lady called Daphne Rye, it probably would never have had a slap-up London production. Miss Rye was at that time casting director for H.M. Tennent Ltd, and came to the last performances at the Arts. Indeed on tickets supplied, but not I think paid for, by me. She was lyrical in her praise for the entire evening, and hastened off to Mr 'Binkie' Beaumont, the astute head of the firm, to persuade him to buy it lock, stock and barrel for the West End.

'What's it about, Daphne dear?' he is reported to have asked.

'Well,' said Daphne, 'it's about a witch who isn't a witch who falls in love with a man who wants to be hanged.'

'Ye-e-e-e-es,' said Binkie, 'And then what, dear?'

'They spend the night in the gaol, and are let off the next morning.'

'It doesn't sound very dramatic,' said Binkie. 'Is there a surprise twist at the end?'

'Oh yes, there's an old rag-and-bone man called Skipps who has nothing to do with anything and comes on trailing a lot of cans, dead drunk, and it's all marvellous and ends happily.'

When further pressed about the plot, she is said to have burst into tears, because she couldn't explain why she had loved it. So that was that. But nothing daunted, Miss Rye got hold of a script and sent it to John Gielgud, who was just back from a long season in America and was about to have one of his rare failures with a revival of *The Return of the Prodigal*. He was enchanted by the Fry play, and decided (I believe, against every advice) to play the leading part and co-direct it with Esmé Percy. Having embarked on the production, he rather wanted to make a clean sweep, but Christopher Fry insisted on Frank Napier and, luckily, me being retained. The tragedy was that Frank died before the production, and was robbed of what I am certain would have been a notable success, ensuring him a lasting niche in the theatre. For me, there will never be another Chaplain, though the late Eliot Makeham, who eventually played it, was very good indeed. But Frank, who was desperately ill when he played it at the Arts, gave it an unearthly quality which was unique. When he said the line 'I am not really here, you know,' it brought the house down, but it was a laugh made more poignant to us by the fact that he almost wasn't there himself. He was in great pain, and I can still see him sitting like a great big black bat at the side of the stage at the Arts, all through the interval, because he couldn't face the stairs up to his dressing-room.

I was frankly terrified of working with John Gielgud, and it was quite clear that in those days he was pretty bored by frightened actors. But it was my first major part in the West End and my morale was not very high. Oh, those rehearsals! Sir John has a quicksilver brain, and chops and changes so many things in one rehearsal that you have no time to write it down until afterwards, and soon your script looks like a patchwork quilt. Most of the company were reduced to tears at some period, and one member succumbed to jaundice and disappeared into the night. Anything I had done at the Arts was ruthlessly exorcised, and I had to fall back on my lines which, it must be admitted, were very fine indeed. I also was helped enormously by having a dear friend in the cast, namely, Miss Pamela Brown, who was now playing the *soi-disant* witch.

Miss B. had been in my Perranporth company for two seasons and had added great lustre thereto. She was now technically a 'star' owing to her zonking success as Claudia, a character I am sure she despised to the roots of her being. Jennet Jourdemayne was a different cup of tea and she played it most beautifully. During the war Christopher Fry had produced her in many plays at the Oxford Playhouse, and as she had worked with Gielgud, frequently to their mutual benefit, this part of the production went pretty smoothly. Pam is the opposite of most leading ladies, in that she rarely speaks unless she has something worth saying and can on occasions be very witty indeed. She was once rung by a famous management, who asked:

'Pamela, could you do Hedda Gabler very quickly at the Lyric, Hammersmith?'

There was a short pause.

'Do you mean SPEAK it very quickly?' asked Miss Brown.

Among her favourite roles, she confesses, are long parts in films which require the minimum of speaking but which lurk in the background on a daily rate and look enigmatic for weeks on end. Her contributions to *The Tales of Hoffman* and *Richard III* thus suited her admirably. It is reported that Sir Laurence Olivier rang her up quite tentatively about the latter. The role he had in mind was Lady Jane Shore, a key part in the production, but he had his doubts about her accepting it owing to the paucity of dialogue.

'You see, Pam, the trouble is that there aren't any lines,' he said.

'NO LINES?' shouted Miss Brown down the blower.

'No, I'm afraid not,' said Sir Laurence, abashed.

'Snap,' said Miss Brown quietly.

However, in *The Lady's Not for Burning* she was to speak a great many lines for months on end. She was to make an enormous impression both in London and New York, and few people who witnessed the piece will forget her first entrance past the window, with red hair flying, and her sinking exhausted on to the floor after being pursued through the town by the angry populace. The action of the play took place 'around the fourteenth century', and for some reason Oliver Messel's most beautiful set unfortunately had no proper exit through the centre door. Owing to the realistic perspective of the backcloth, those involved in the second act could not creep off to their dressing-rooms and therefore had to pretend that they were going off into the adjoining room and in fact do just that. The only difficulty was that the room they went into was in reality a cubby-hole in which Harcourt Williams (the Mayor), Eliot Makeham (Chaplain), Richard Leech (who played the lecherous brother, Humphrey), and I had to sit for all of twenty minutes while Miss Brown and Sir John played a very long love scene. For the first few weeks I listened to it sometimes (and this is not affectation), being so moved that I used to wet my peepers, but later on we fell back on our own devices through boredom. And it was quite a surprise to the audience when one night the door flew open to disclose the Messrs Leech and Bull deep in an acrimonious game of chess, Eliot Makeham reading a rather lurid thriller, and Harcourt Williams plainly doing the *Daily Telegraph* crossword. The young lovers were played by Richard Burton and Claire Bloom, and it is certain that this production set them both on the road to fame. Richard clearly had an exceptional talent. His sincerity and physical beauty were deeply impressive, and when he scrubbed the floor during the long love scene before mentioned, it was obvious that a new star was in embryo, even on his knees.

The remainder of the Mayor's family were played by Nora Nicholson, who brought wit and acerbity to the wife, and David Evans (Nicholas), who had a corncrake voice which issued out of a small compact body with droll results. I shared a dressing-room with him for over a year and we never exchanged a cross word which is, I believe, a European record. Esmé Percy played the rag-and-bone man, Skipps, and he was a bit worrying to act with, as he had a knack of never giving remotely the same performance. He had a unique personality and was a very lovable man of great sweetness and a marvellous raconteur. I can only hope that he has regaled the angels in heaven with the tale of the Tuesday matinée at Leeds when his glass eye fell out through his exuberance. We were all conscious of his affliction, and in moments of supreme bad taste had made suggestions of what we would do if an accident occurred. These varied from breaking into a song and dance to the tune 'You've Got Your Eye On Me', to turning the play into one about Nelson quite suddenly.

But when it actually happened, we were all thunderstruck and quite incapable of even going on with the play. There was Esmé hopping about, looking for the damned thing which had slid down my capacious robe and fallen tinkling to the ground. It was simply no help Esmé whispering to the world in general, 'Don't tread on it. It cost eight guineas.' If it had cost 8,000 guineas, I doubt if I could have uprooted myself from my particular spot. Finally, Richard Leech found it and returned it to the owner, but after all, as we said to each other afterwards in Fullers (black coffee with the Buck Rarebits after that ordeal), he (Richard) was still a fully qualified doctor. The trouble was that it was the first of many similar incidents, and Oliver Messel had designed a beautiful patch for Esmé, who looked like a dear rather artistic pirate in it.

But I am anticipating more than somewhat and the Leeds incident occurred quite late in the pre-London tour, which was interminable and at some points downright disheartening. The provincial audiences seemed not to be able to make head or tail of the play. Only in Newcastle and Birmingham did we find real warmth and appreciation and a faint hope that disaster did not lie in wait for us in London, and many's the time the management and Sir John must have felt like calling the whole thing off. We reached the nadir of depression at Northampton where we played Holy Week to a stony silence. Apart from a visit to the Boot Museum (v. sinister), it was not a happy time and the New Theatre's policy did not help our morale. For, due to follow us as an attraction, was a Variety Show featuring 'Real Frogmen in a Real Tank' and the front of the theatre was plastered with pictures of the daring gentlemen. So obscured were the details of our piece that one patron left the theatre in a rage shouting, 'If they advertise frogmen I want to see frogmen,' and didn't even wait till the last act to see if one popped up. We did suggest to Esmé that he might play Skipps as a rag-and-frogman, but he declined.

All through the tour we rehearsed incessantly and the company did get to know and love one another, but I think everyone was astounded at the warmth of the reception when we finally opened at the Globe Theatre, on 11 May 1949. It was evident from the moment the curtain went up that for once a first-night audience had come to enjoy themselves and with a unanimous press we were in for a very long run.

But we were never allowed to get stale, mainly because Sir John Gielgud is a perfectionist and keeps on altering a production which he has directed. If he is appearing in the play as well, one has no chance of slacking, as his eyes are all over the place, and many's the time he would change an entire scene between a matinée and evening performance.

'I think you're getting a bit stale, Peter,' he would remark of a Saturday just before the evening performance. 'Try playing the last scene from the opposite side of the stage.'

I would remonstrate half-heartedly, knowing he was right, take a nip of brandy before going on for the scene and make a hash of it.

'Sorry. Go back to the old way,' would say Sir John after the perf. But he had scored his point and one became more alert. There was a pretty extraordinary evening when he wanted all those hidden behind the door in the second act to burst out with more excitement and dash, making up exclamations as they ran. Even the old hands, the Messrs Williams and Makeham, boggled a bit at this.

'Couldn't we rehearse it once?' they asked.

'No,' said Sir John, 'it will spoil the excitement.'

So that evening out we came with more excitement and dash than you would believe possible. But unfortunately a series of mishaps were to befall which negatived the effect. Both Harcourt Williams and Eliot Makeham, by some strange coincidence, let out an identical exclamation, which plunged them into hysterics. I collided with Richard Leech, who knocked into Pamela Brown, who collapsed on the floor. As it was only a few minutes before she was meant to faint dead away, this was not going to help the plot. Suddenly I caught sight of Richard Burton who had stopped scrubbing the floor to stare at us with glazed horror. As he had had no warning of the change, he thought we had taken leave of our senses.

'Sorry, chaps,' muttered Sir John, 'entirely my fault,' as the curtain fell and we all dissolved into more helpless laughter. No wonder we were all potty about him, and as far as I am concerned he personifies the theatre at its highest and most noble. His enthusiasm and energy are boundless, and though he can be a hard taskmaster, most of the results are worth it. He has a notoriously quick tongue which has caused him to drop enough 'bricks' to build a National Theatre.

A typical one was when we made a recording of the play during the New York run. The following evening I popped into his dressing-room.

'Oh, Peter, you were quite good in the recording,' said my hero, but the emphasis was so much on the last word that it gave me a saddening clue as to what he had thought of my stage performance for the past eighteen months.

During the run I had the honour to be asked by him to be in a scene from *Richard of Bordeaux*, in which he was to play his original part for a special charity 'do' at the Coliseum.

'Would you play the Archbishop of York, Peter?' he asked, and as an afterthought said, 'You see, you can wear your *Lady's Not for Burning* costume,' which took a little of the gilt off the gingerbread, I must admit.

Sir John was going to do the last scene of the play and Richard Burton was to play the faithful Maudelyn. Richard Leech, Harcourt Williams and I supported them. *Richard of Bordeaux* had been Sir John's first great success in the commercial theatre at the New Theatre in 1933. We rehearsed in the Globe and I shan't easily forget the first time we read it. Sir John sat in a chair wearing a hat and reading from a script. Suddenly he threw hat and script away and played the rest of the scene word-perfect with tears rolling down his cheeks. We were moved to speechlessness and very near tears ourselves. In fact, the whole thing was a bit weepy, even though David Evans said, with a certain amount of cause, that I looked like a cross between Superman and Blériot flying the Channel. I think this simile was due to a rather unsuitable hat. But the performance provided plenty of thrills, and it's the only time I've been on a stage while a fellow-artist brought the house down. And that's what Sir John did. After the scene we made our way through all the chorus ladies of London, who were waiting to go on and beat the hell out of *There's No Business Like Show Business*, and they parted like the Red Sea to let Sir John through. With glistening eyes he turned to us and said: 'Thanks, chaps; well, we had a jolly good blub anyhow.'

At the beginning of 1949 the last weeks of *The Lady's Not for Burning* were announced in spite of the continued good business, but Sir John was due at Stratford-on-Avon. There were rumours of an American production, but it obviously would not take place till the autumn.

I filled in the gap with TVs, an occasional film and a bizarre production of *Pericles* and in September we started rehearsing for *The Lady* again. There were two changes in the cast: George Howe took over from Harcourt Williams, and a talented young actress called Penelope Munday played Alison. Claire Bloom was released to play in *Ring Round the Moon*, another bull's-eye for Christopher Fry who adapted it.

The opening in New York at the Royale Theatre on 8 November 1950, was a curious experience, because whereas they had laughed generously at the play in Boston and been obviously intrigued by it, the New Yorkers at the three public previews sat as quiet as mice and never made a movement. We were depressed and thought we were in for a disaster, and the actual first-night crowd were not much better except for dear faithful Hermione Gingold, who laughed loud and long at all HER favourite jokes, which didn't seem to coincide with those of the rest of the audience. We took several curtain calls, but it wasn't till the rave notices in the papers next morning that we realized we were a hit. In New York you must have favourable reviews in the two main papers, the *Times* and the *Herald Tribune* or you might as well close the building, even if ALL the other papers are mad about you. Also, there is no such thing in the theatre there as 'word of mouth', and many's the play with a great deal of appeal for the general public which has vanished overnight in a welter of critical disdain.

The net result of the notices was fascinating. The second performance was strangely enough a matinée and a riot at that. Old ladies fell tumbling into the aisles, and it was obvious that now they knew it was a comedy, they could be permitted to enjoy themselves. I settled down happily in a strange hotel called the Henry Hudson, which had a swimming-pool, three restaurants and an anglophile director called John Paul Stack who had a mania for old English cars. I had a tiny room on the twenty-first floor with a balcony which gave me a magical view of New York. There were plenty of shows to see and every Sunday night there was a benefit performance of one of the successes for charity, which was a splendid idea. Pam Brown and I managed to get enough seats for *Guys and Dolls* to give them as Christmas presents to the company. One of my biggest thrills was meeting many of the *New Yorker* contributors in the apartment of my idol, Charles Addams. A striking feature of his home was a glass case of the type in which most people keep their china, but his case was dedicated to model guillotines, gallowses and lethal weapons.

A good many droll things happened both on and off the stage. For instance, there was the night when Miss Brown said that her father was 'Lost in the soup' instead of 'Lost in a search', which only registered on her and Sir John several seconds later. Then there was the night of the biggest laugh of the run. It occurred after the curtain had been up on the third act for a few minutes, and the audience noisily dissolved into hysterics. As no one had said anything remotely funny, the Messrs Gielgud, Evans and Leech had a quick look at their costumes to see if anything had split and tried to get on with the scene. It was not until they had got into the wings that they were told that the coloured commissionaire, who usually stood outside the Royale Theatre, had wandered backstage to give a message, had lost his way, and popped his dark becapped head through Mayor Tyson's window. It is possible that the audience thought that it was another inspired quirk of Christopher Fry's, but unfortunately he couldn't be bribed to do it again.

Then there was the laughable incident of Miss Brown's photograph. One night after the show some of us had visited an amusement arcade and gone into one of those booths where you have your photograph taken and developed while you wait. Miss Brown had bought an enchanting hat, and I suggested that she should have some pictures taken of her in it. I took her the next night to the same booth and was rather bossy with my experience of the machine. I told her not to move while the light was on and in what direction to look. I put the twenty-five cents into the machine, and Miss Brown sat there still and radiant in her new hat. When the light went out I told her she could relax, and stood by waiting for the finished result. The photograph came through into the slot after a minute and I took one look and handed it to her.

'Think you must have moved,' I commented. On the photograph was a lady with a bare behind in Russian boots. We laughed till the tears rolled down our cheeks and up to this very date no satisfactory explanation can be found. Whether some manufacturer of pornography had been caught in the act and had to leave before the results of his or her labour, or whether it had been placed there as a joke, I shall never know; but it became the Great Photo Mystery for the cast of *The Lady's Not for Burning* for many a long day.

Backstage at the Royale was fairly sordid. I was amazed at the squalor of the dressing-rooms, and even our oldest theatres compare favourably with those in New York. Under the tables there was vintage chewing-gum, the doorkeeper was impersonal and never there, and the approach to the stage door became inches under water when the weather was inclement. We shared the passage with two other companies, one of which was *South Pacific*, and it was quite a usual sight to see the exquisite Mary Martin wade through into her theatre. She paid us the compliment of slipping across several times during her waits and watching bits of our play from the wings.

During the run we were all engaged for a radio version of *Hamlet* for the Theatre Guild of the Air. Sir John kindly worked us all into it, and it was a strange experience, as I had never realized the incredible carry-on connected with these productions. There was a last public run-through in a packed theatre, there were introductions of all the artistes, who had to bow to the audience, and a ruthless cutting of the play down to an hour and a quarter in order to enable someone to bang on about United States Steel. Since then, of course, I have worked for commercial TV, but somehow one does not get personally involved in the commercial aspect. Sir John sailed through it all calmly and with such dignity that we were all immensely proud of him.

At the end of the New York run we played a fortnight in both Washington and Philadelphia. In the former we played at a very old-fashioned theatre indeed called the National, with a restricted depth to the stage. I have put this bit of information in because Sir John told the Messrs Howe, Makeham, Leech and myself that he was very sorry, but just for this week we would have to stay on the stage behind the door during the second act love scene. We did not have the heart to tell him that we had been doing this for the last eighteen months anyhow.

In Philadelphia some of us stayed in a remarkably unconventional hotel which reached a new high in sordidity, but we were only charged fifteen dollars a week. To our delight some of the Burlesque Theatre ladies were staying there too. They clocked in on the Sunday night and were doing stripteases at 0001 hours on Monday morning, to conform with the laws of the city. They were hard-working girls and their show was of course delightfully old-fashioned. In another theatre in this city we saw a musical called *A Tree Grows in Brooklyn* with an unforgettable performance by Shirley Booth, which shone like an opal, warm, glittering and true.

Regretfully we all parted company in New York at the end of April and went our several ways. I took off for California for an extraordinary three months, which now seems like a bad dream. I went to stay with the Grangers and nearly landed parts in both *Rommel* and *Androcles and the Lion*. However, I did not in fact work at all, and indeed spent most of my savings. I cannot regard it as a complete waste of time owing to what I learned about life in Hollywood (second instalment); I think all this knowledge is stored away safely somewhere, but I can only remember ridiculous things about this visit.

I recall vividly trying with Mr Granger to save the lives of his goldfish, who were suffocating from the mud (symbolic, as I said to Mr G.). Then there was Gabriel Pascal's swimming-pool, which was exactly like the one Miss Swanson possessed in *Sunset Boulevard*, though there were leaves at the bottom of Pascal's instead of persons. Other things to remember were the looks on everyone's faces when Jean Simmons announced at a smartish party that she'd been playing tennis on the Santa Monica Public Courts for free, Peter Glenville's yells when he thought he'd been attacked by a tarantula in Gladys Cooper's house, and Marlene Dietrich destroying my illusions in one night by eating vast quantities of hamburgers and sauerkraut in Hamburger Heaven. To counteract all this there was the hospitality and kindness dispensed by George Cukor and others and above all the unchanging face and nature of Miss Jean Simmons.

Apart from this, Hollywood seemed a morass of unhappy and insecure people with a layer of masks over their faces and souls which were not worth uncovering – and anyhow you can read all this sort of stuff in any of the novels about the celluloid city. I came home with very little money and three stone lighter in weight. This had been achieved by stringent dieting and ghastly exercises, in order that I might amaze my friends and relations who had been convinced that I would come back swollen considerably. It also enabled me to tackle my first job on my return, which was, ironically, to play the heavyweight wrestling champion of the world on TV.

7
Waiting for Godot

It all began during that lovely, lovely summer of 1955; I was minding my own business and quietly enjoying the sun at the Oasis and Serpentine swimming-pools, when a phone call came from the Arts Theatre. A Mr Peter Hall wanted me to read a play called *Waiting for Godot*. He was away in Spain at the time, but had left word that he hoped for a speedy decision. Whatever the play was like, it needed time to consider the pros and cons, because although I was in my usual parlous state of penury, the prospects of a few weeks' work at the Club theatre didn't exhilarate. You are (or were) paid twelve pounds a week and nothing at all for rehearsals (four weeks), though you were presented with a sheaf of tickets with which to purchase luncheon at the snack bar. An additional liability is that friends wishing to see the piece invariably have to get you to get them tickets, as you have been made an Honorary Member. If you are in a very popular play they rally round like flies and if you aren't frightfully good, forget to come round after the performance and pay for their seats. This is a double disappointment.

But, and it is a big But, some of the productions there have enormous prestige value and do one a lot of good professionally: viz. *The Lady's Not for Burning.* Contrariwise I had also played there in a sensational flop called *Second Best Bed*, which was the Coronation offering of the little theatre. A gentle satire on W. Shakespeare's courtship of the late Miss Hathaway, it incurred the wrath of critics and audience alike.

So on receiving the script of *Waiting for Godot*, I had one hit and one miss as precedent. I also found myself totally incapable of making any sort of decision after reading the play for the first time, which was in itself an extraordinary experience. I thought either the author or I must be potty, and yet even at first reading there was a hypnotic quality about the dialogue which could not be lightly dismissed. But I could not begin to understand what my proposed role (Pozzo) meant, and in consequence decided to turn it down, as I considered it pointless to contemplate playing a part through which I could see no daylight. I had hardly turned it down before I received a charming letter from Peter Hall asking me to reconsider the play and diabolically suggesting that I was ideal for the part. It was so cleverly phrased that I was completely won over to the idea, though even when I had agreed to have a shot at it, I stipulated that, if I felt unhappy in the part after a few days' rehearsal, I could leave. The fact that I felt unhappy months after playing it has nothing to do with this point. We were to start practising the first week of July and I looked forward to it with alarm and despondency.

The original cast was composed of Paul Daneman, Timothy Bateson, Peter Woodthorpe and myself. The only one I knew nothing about was P. Woodthorpe, who was a discovery from the Cambridge Footlights Company and drove us all barking mad at the beginning. It was infuriating in my case (my silver wedding with the theatre had just been celebrated) to find an amateur actor with more talent than oneself, acting one off the stage, and his seeming confidence and technique struck an impertinent note. It was also a bit galling to discover that he hadn't yet made up his mind as to whether to go back to the University for his final year or continue to play with us. He was at any rate a 'natural', and I've rarely seen such incredible promise. Timothy Bateson was fairly new to me, though vastly more experienced, and I remember him playing very old gents and young things at the Old Victoria Music Hall and with Sir Laurence and Lady O in all those *Cleopatras*. As we were to remain tied to each other throughout the engagement, it was essential that we should remain on friendly terms, and in this we succeeded admirably and I found his acidity and wit helped me enormously throughout a depressing run.

Paul Daneman played Vladimir (one of the two tramps) only at the

Arts and gave a wonderful performance, tinged with great compassion
and simplicity. He was a tower of strength and a joy to work with. To
complete the cast was a small boy, and the young actor playing this
part had to be constantly whisked out of the theatre, when the
'Dirty' bits were being spoken. He also had to be changed periodically,
owing to the LCC laws regarding stage children. The result of this
was a caterpillar of young gents of varying talent and disposition.
One with the face of an angel could be heard from one end of the
theatre to the other hurling very adult epithets at his mother.
Rehearsals started soberly, and I took an instant liking to the young
director Peter Hall, who made no bones about the play.

'Haven't really the foggiest idea what some of it means,' he
announced cheerfully, 'but if we stop and discuss every line we'll
never open. I think it may be dramatically effective but there's no
hope of finding out till the first night.'

There was certainly no assistance coming from the author Mr
Samuel Beckett, and looking back on the production, I'm rather glad
he didn't put in an appearance till quite late in the run. The
rehearsals were the most gruelling that I've ever experienced in all
my puff. The lines were baffling enough, but the props that I was
required to carry about my person made life intolerable. Aspiring
actors are hereby warned against parts that entail them being tied to
another artiste, as they will find it restricts their movements. As
well as this handicap I had to carry an overcoat, a giant watch, a pipe,
lorgnettes and heaven knows what else. The rope had to be adjusted
continuously, so that I could pull it taut round my slave's neck, if
possible not throttling Mr Bateson (Lucky was the name of the
character). Fortunately there were long duologues between the
tramps, so while they rehearsed on the stage proper, Master Bateson
and I could have a bash in the Oak Room of the Arts Club, until
complaints came up, via the head-waiter from the restaurant below,
about the noise and general banging about.

I found it frightfully difficult to get any sense out of my intended
characterization, until the last week of rehearsals, when I suddenly
decided to cheat and pretend Miss Margaret Rutherford was playing
the role, which had the immediate and blessed effect of stopping

embarrassing myself. It is a platitude to say that when an actor embarrasses himself, he is bound to embarrass the audience. I had noticed that my friends were clearly mortified at having to hear my lines, and Bob Morley had thrown the script from one end of his garden to the other, when I had unwisely asked him to take me through the part. The dress rehearsals were gloomy affairs and not relieved for yours truly by the physical discomforts of wearing a wig constructed of rubber, in the middle of a heatwave. Owing to the author's eccentricity it was necessary for Pozzo to take his bowler-hat off at one stage of the piece and reveal a completely naked head. This was symbolic (the only explanation for the nightly torture given to me) and then he put his titfer on again. It was only for a second or two, but proved to be one of my major miseries. A firm of wig makers, Wig Creations Ltd, had constructed for me what amounted to a bathing-cap, which had to be encased in rubber solution. This caused an *impasse* when dry, owing to lack of air in the hair, and by the end of any performance there were several pints of not madly attractive sweat accumulated in the rubber wig, which made one feel as if one's head had burst. Later in the run I contracted a series of skin diseases as a result and had to issue a *pronunciamento*. The consequence was that a new type of bathing-cap was dished out, not so chic, as it had a few wisps of hair at the back, which meant that I did not have to seal off my head completely. The whole thing was pretty preposterous because, as Mr R. Morley kindly pointed out, the wig-join was clearly visible from Row K in the stalls. Make-up has never been my *forte*, and in this case the earlier I came in to do it, the more frightening seemed to be the result. I used to arrive some two hours before my first entrance in *Godot*, and by the time I reached the stage, the rubber started to come unstuck, which resulted in *ditto* for my performance. If I ever got held up by necessity or accident and got into the theatre late, I was always able to put on a superb make-up in ten minutes flat!

The first night was, I think, my most alarming experience on the stage (so far). I have a habit of comforting myself on first nights by trying to think of appalling experiences during the war, when terror struck from all sides, but the windiness felt on the Italian beachheads and elsewhere was nothing to compare with one's panic on that evening of 3 August 1955, and why the cast were not given medals for gallantry in the face of the enemy is inexplicable. Waves of hostility came whirling over the footlights, and the mass exodus, which was to form such a feature of the run of the piece, started quite soon after the curtain had risen. The audible groans were also fairly disconcerting. By the time I had to make my first entrance (twenty minutes after the rise of the curtain) I realized that I was in for a sticky evening and I'm not referring to my rubber wig. The laughs had been few and far between and there was a general air of restlessness and insecurity around. I lost my head quite early on by inserting the rope, to which Mr Bateson was attached to me, INSIDE my coat sleeve. Knowing what I do now and how the audience were never surprised by anything that happened during *Godot*, I should have just said, 'Pig, put my coat on properly, pig,' which was the endearing form of address that I habitually used to my slave.

As it was, I spent the next quarter of an hour in a semi-hysterical condition, knowing that if I hadn't actually strangled Mr Bateson by the time he got to his big speech, it was highly probable that he would have to make it in pitch darkness owing to non-arrival at the position on which his spotlight was trained. As it was Mr Bateson's big moment, I hazarded a guess that he might not be best pleased. I gradually eased the rope up my sleeve in order to reduce the danger, but at the expense of my performance, which had by now been reduced to a question of survival without having heart failure. I was blowing the audience out of the auditorium with the volume of my shrill voice – (quote Kenneth Tynan) 'over-vocalization' (unquote) which was the understatement of the year. But T. Bateson got his light, declaimed his gibberish and brought the house down with terrifying accuracy.

After this the audience were a little more attentive, and though an occasional groan or rudely upturned seat rang through the building, we got through without disaster. I pulled myself together in the second act and the Messrs Daneman and Woodthorpe were very moving indeed in the last scene of all. The curtain fell to mild applause, we took a scant three calls and a depression and sense of anti-climax descended on us all. Very few people came round, and most of those who did were in a high state of intoxication and made even less sense than the play. I slipped quietly away with the Scofields and Maurice Kaufmann, who had all promised to pick up the bits.

The notices next day were almost uniformly unfavourable, confused and unprovocative. We played to poor houses, but on the Sunday following our opening the whole picture was to change. We quite suddenly became the rage of London, a phenomenon entirely due to the articles written by the Messrs Tynan and Hobson in the *Observer* and *Sunday Times* respectively. One phrase quoted from each doyen of criticism was enough to send all London running to the Arts and subsequently the Criterion Theatres. Mr Hobson said, 'Something that will securely lodge in a corner of your mind as long as you live,' and Mr Tynan told his readers that 'it will be a conversational necessity for many years to have seen *Waiting for Godot*'. With no mock humility I have to report that Mr H. also said, 'This Bull's bellow troubles the memory like the swansong of humanity,' but I fancy Mr Derek Granger in the *Financial Times* was nearer the mark when he said I looked like a 'vast obscene baby'.

That Sunday night we played to near capacity and the whole trend of audience behaviour was to alter for the remainder of the run at the Arts. Gusts of laughter and tense silences greeted our efforts, and people started to come round to tell us what They thought the play meant. There were rumours even of a transfer, but in the meantime our run was extended. Mr Hobson mentioned the play every week in his columns, and we were suddenly informed that Mr Donald Albery, who owned the rights of *Godot* anyhow, had arranged with his father Sir Bronson Albery to take us to the Criterion Theatre. This was a real turn-up for the book, as this delicious little house is a dream emporium for the actor's wares from every angle. It has what is known as a marvellous 'passing' trade, is easily accessible and a wonderful theatre to play in. The only disadvantage lies in conditions backstage, which are nobody's fault, but at first sight one might easily be in the sewers of Paris. It is chronically airless and there are mixed pongs coming from the restaurants and kitchens above. Owing to the smallness of the cast we were able to have a largish dressing-room to ourselves, and after a slight argument with Mr Albery about billing, I signed the contract.

I hoped it would sound a bit grand, that last bit about billing I mean. It wasn't actually and I merely happened to ask my agent to arrange that I should be billed after Hugh Burden, who was taking over the part of Vladimir from Paul Daneman who was about to go into the ill-fated *Punch Revue* at the Duke of York's. I didn't ask for neon lights or red letters eight foot high or anything, but Mr Albery said there was no question of order of billing, as he exercised the right to have the names of actors on the bills or NOT. He was absolutely correct and in order, but I did point out (through my agent) that there would not be much point, having performed anonymously at the Arts Theatre, in doing *ditto* at Piccadilly Circus, the Centre of the World. We came to a midget *impasse* and I decided not to rehearse for a few days until things were settled. I popped off to the Oasis swimming-pool, while he made up his mind whether to replace me. Fortunately for me he decided against that and I returned browner, and I fear smugger, to rehearse.

We opened in the second week of September and were to run continuously till the end of the following March. It was the oddest theatrical experience of my life and had a nightmarish quality that is difficult to recapture in words. Both physically and mentally it was a disturbing play with which to be associated. The bleakness and sordidity of the set and the clothes, the spitting and drooling that formed part of the pattern, had a most depressing effect on me and I came to dread going to the theatre. I also found, as time went on, that I started to disbelieve in the merits of the play and to become more and more intolerant of the praise and importance that were bestowed on it in certain quarters. I got wildly bored by the endless banging-on at parties, in the street and particularly in my dressing-room. But of course it was all this *brouhaha* that helped me to pay my rent for so long.

The High Teas on Saturdays helped a great deal. For me one of the nicest traits in Mr Donald Albery's character is his care of his actors' stomachs, and with a twice-nightly carry-on every Saturday (5.30

and 8.30 perfs), he has instituted a splendid idea in his theatres, whereby a kind lady comes in and serves delicious cold-cuts and coffee between the two shows at enormous expense to Mr A. The actors can then lollop away to their dressing-rooms with a plate and make pigs of themselves. It was a bit tricky when friends came round between shows, but one could usually find a bone to toss to them. In any case I kept a widow's cruse of brandy handy, not only for myself, but for those customers stalwart enough to stay the course.

It must be admitted that a lot of people didn't, and it was a remarkable thing to come on in the first act and feel a bungful house, only to return in the second to find a certain percentage of gaps in the theatre and the audience shrunk in size. Not that it was a great surprise, because those who had left did not attempt to cover up their movements. It was not just the banging of seats and slamming of exit doors, but quite often they would take the trouble to come right down to the footlights, glare at the actors and make their egress into outer space, snorting the while. Incidents were numerous and cries of 'Rubbish', 'It's a disgrace', 'Take it off', 'Disgusting', and I regret to say on one occasion 'Balls', floated through the auditorium. There was one unforgettable night when, during the second act, the two tramps are alone on the stage cogitating about life as they were apt to do and one says: 'I am happy,' to which the other replies, 'I am happy too,' after which a gent in Row F shouted: 'Well, I'm bloody well not.'

At this point there was a certain amount of shushing, but the man would not be shushed and stood up and yelled at the audience: 'And nor are you. You've been hoaxed like me.'

A free fight ensued (well, fairly free; 15s. 6d. a head actually) and during a lull Hugh Burden observed quietly:

'I think it's Godot,' which brought the house down and enabled our attendants to get rid of the angry middle-aged man.

But perhaps the drollest night was when I got my come-uppance. It had been reported to me by the stage manager that a party of eight had arrived rather late, and had made a good deal of noise sitting down in the front row. They were all in full evening dress with a fine display of jewels and/or carnations. By the time I'd been on for a bit I realized that they didn't seem best pleased by me or my performance. The muttering and whispering grew to a crescendo, until in a loud clear voice the dowager lady seated in the middle of the party said:

'I do wish the fat one would go.'

I took a hurried look round at my fellow actors and decided that I had never seen a thinner bunch and guessed that she must be referring to me. I was a fraction shocked as, after a long and not terribly notable career in the service of the theatre, I have never actually been insulted DURING a performance. People have attacked me in the streets or in public transport, but never while I was actually doing it. I seethed inwardly with rage, but apart from glaring at the lady I was unable to make a come-back; luckily my beloved slave made handsome amends. As we were about to leave the stage, I shortened the rope which bound me to T. Bateson and he made as if to leap into the lady's lap, a threat which caused the entire party to leave hurriedly. Afterwards we were all filled with intense compassion and the milk of h.k., as it turned out that the party had arrived expecting to see a revue called *Intimacy at 8.30* which had vacated the Criterion Theatre a few weeks previously. Putting one and five together and realizing the storm of criticism that would assail her at the end of the evening, the hostess had wisely decided to cut her losses.

Of course a lot of people were blackmailed into coming to *Godot* by the quotes in the press plastered outside the theatre and in the newspaper columns. It was no good expecting to find 'one of the funniest plays in London' if two tramps wrangling for a couple of hours on a stage, naked except for a leafless tree, wasn't your idea of a gay evening out. Then there were those who thought they wouldn't be asked out ANYWHERE if they hadn't seen it, thanks to Mr Tynan's pronouncement about it being a 'conversational necessity'. Sometimes I longed to stop prospective customers streaming up to the box-office and try and divert them to *Dry Rot* at the Whitehall Theatre, though I fancy a lot of them thought they had been seeing the latter anyhow.

But theatrical London did flock to it, and in consequence the piece did one's reputation a great deal of good, though a lot of members of the profession were not strong enough to stay the course. Early in the run my phone rang one morning and it was Mr R. Morley on the other end.

'Guess who was in front last night?' he asked.

'Boris Karloff,' I replied correctly.

'AND me,' he said, hurt. 'At least, for the first act,' he added. 'But I told the people I was with that there was no point in staying for the second, as it was exactly the same apart from you being dumb in it.'

I told him coldly that I was blind in the second act, and that I had troubled Mr Harold Hobson's memory 'like the swan-song of humanity', but Mr Morley could not be tempted to return, and indeed his memory was so troubled that he used to ring me up periodically and mutter on the phone:

'I've been brooding in my bath, and it is my considered opinion that the success of *Waiting for Godot* is the end of the theatre as we know it.'

The author left his Montparnasse lair and visited us round about the hundredth performance and proved to be shy, modest and not frightfully helpful about the meaning of his play. We got the impression that he didn't care for the London production a great deal. He gave us a party, where we were all rather rude to him, but he took it in good part, and left for France after telling us that he didn't think the pauses quite long enough.

We rang down on 24 March 1956, after last-minute attempts at a transfer had failed. I packed my rubber wig away for the last time (or so I thought), and heaved a gigantic sigh of relief. I thought of thanking Mr Donald Albery publicly, by taking a small column in *The Stage*, and announcing: 'Mr Peter Bull thanks Mr Donald Albery for a lucrative but not frightfully enjoyable engagement,' but decided wisely against it.

No one seemed madly anxious to employ me, and instead of going away, I hung about London trying to get a move on with my second book. My first, *To Sea in a Sieve*, had come out on 27 February, and to my amazement was bringing in some splendid dividends. It was then that a new vista opened. Perhaps I'd be able, in a few years' time, to retire from the stage to a lovely cottage in Kent with roses and paperbacks littering the place, and a lot of old photographs of scenes from *Waiting for Godot*. But it was not to be yet. Suddenly, a Mr Michael Wide rang me up to ask if I would consider going out on a tour of *Waiting for Godot*. I told him he must be out of his tiny mind, and he said, oh no, he hoped to make a lot of money. He added then that Timothy Bateson and Peter Woodthorpe had said they'd do it if I did. I was frankly flabbergasted by the whole project, but suddenly thinking that it might be the funniest tour ever organized, I said I would. I asked for a percentage (knowing that the 'returns' would ensure one good laugh per evening and certainly per matinée) and an armed guard to and from the stage door at the Grand Theatre, Blackpool, a wise precaution as you will see.

It was to be an eight weeks' tour, and at the end of the sixth I could give notice to quit. Three of the dates were in the London suburbs, so topographically it could not be so ghastly. It would also enable me to save a bit against my holiday which I was determined to take that year. Robert Eddison was to play Vladimir and Richard Scott was to direct. Rehearsals were held in the Chelsea Community Centre (handy for me, living just down the road), and I fear nice Mr Scott, who had hoped to give the play an entirely new production, was a bit disappointed to find that the gallant survivors not only wouldn't but couldn't alter their performance. It was a cause of *sauve qui peut*, and I was only concerned for Robert who had the heavy end to carry. But he rose triumphantly to the occasion and went confidently and quietly about his business.

We opened at the Coliseum Theatre, Harrow, on 21 May 1956, a house of entertainment we practically closed down. A few weeks later it was reconstructed into apartment houses. It was not an auspicious opening date, as the theatre resembled a tunnel, and back-stage conditions were bleak. There was no doorkeeper, no call-boy and no audience to speak of or even speak back. But we were able to get back to our respective homes in the evening and there was a frequent train service. I don't think any of the Harrovians slipped out of their dorms to 'get the message', and it was only during this week that we discovered to our huge delight that Michael Wide's principal backer was none other than Miss Winifred Atwell, the ebullient and talented coloured boogie-woogie pianist. So this made it all right somehow. Her husband, who was also her business manager, used to ring up every evening at Harrow to ascertain the figures, and it was fortunate that the phone was between Master Bateson's and my dressing-room, so there was a rush to give them to him. Actually the first twice (if you know what I mean) he could not believe them at all, and when on the Friday we'd nosedived into the fifties, he thought there must be an error and we meant £250 odd. It was lucky that his wife was playing to around the £1,000 mark EVERY performance at that time in the Palladium.

We played to £499 12s 10 1/2d., so the cast did not get very much extra that week, but the Monday following we opened at the Arts Theatre, Cambridge, which was to be quite a different pair of tramps. You would have thought by the laughter, bookings and general behaviour that we had brought the great Laughing Success of the Century to their doors and we played to virtual capacity. The running time went up by fifteen minutes in order to give the audience a chance to get over their apoplectic fits, and dons showed us round their collections of precious glass and things. We were patronized by the local theatre groups, who kindly interrupted their activities for a second to tell us what THEY were doing NEXT season, and Peter Woodthorpe (ex-Footlights star) had a great personal triumph on the stage, in the press, and all over the street, which plunged Timothy and me in an orgy of beastliness to him. He took it in fairly good part and we pressed on to Blackpool.

Miss Atwell and her husband, to say nothing of Mr Wide, had been perked up considerably after the Cambridge week, only to be plunged into gloom by our sensational visit to the Lancashire seaside resort. It was to provide us with some unforgettable memories, and what possessed the management to book us in must be shrouded for ever in mystery. But even this cardinal error was eclipsed by their invitation to the Blackpool Old Age Pensioners to view *Waiting for Godot* at 1s. a head on the Monday night. It was soon apparent that this gesture was not far short of insanity. The OAPS were very angry indeed, after the first few minutes, at not only having to witness *Waiting for Godot*, but also having to pay twelve having to witness *Waiting for Godot*, but also having to pay twelve pennies for the privilege. They determined to have their say, which meant that during the second act we couldn't have ours, so there was a bit of an *impasse*. Bedlam reigned, what with the banging of seats, yells of derision and one or two pertinent remarks when the tramps suggested hanging themselves. We started off with 700 persons in the Grand Theatre, and finished up with under 100. We took one quick curtain and there were rumours of the police being called out for 'our special safety' as it says on some fire curtains. The awful thing is that I rather enjoyed the evening, as I had not needed a clairvoyant to tell me that Blackpool was not going to be one long triumph.

We were to do every penny of £444 on the week and we had a fairly alarming mid-week matinée. The Blackpudlians eyed us more than curiously in the streets, and one felt one should ring a leper's bell on approaching Boots the Cash Chemists to change one's library book. Mark you, the local press went to town about the whole affair (it was slightly out of season anyhow) and rallied to our support. We were front-page news for the entire week. 'Godot went through without interruption' or 'There were two curtain-calls last night at the Grand Theatre' were typical sub-headlines and there was even a 'leader' saying Blackpool didn't DESERVE to be sent shows like us and the Carl Rosa Opera Company, if they were going to behave like this. The truth of the matter was that poor Blackpool didn't deserve *Waiting for Godot*. In a city almost entirely devoted to sex-shows, oysters, plastic macs and the pursuit of pleasure, it was an anachronism to present such a piece there.

By the end of the week we were all a bit nervy and I couldn't wait to get out of the town. Even 'Sex-drugged girls tell all' had turned out to be two giggly nudes. I had had one bad shrimp and been sick on the pier, so I decided to go to London that weekend, whatever the cost. Now to leave Blackpool on a Saturday night is a tricky assignment, as the only chance is to catch the 10.39 out of Preston, a city which lies about fifteen miles out of Blackpool. Well, as the curtain of *Waiting for Godot* in theory didn't come down until 10.15, it was going to be a close shave, to put it mildly. But Master

Bateson, who was taking part in the expedition, and I were by now desperate men and we were not going to be defeated by such a little obstacle as Time. We went to the Messrs Eddison and Woodthorpe, our tramp confederates, and asked them if they would be so kind as to leave out ALL the pauses at the second house on Saturday. Those of you who saw the play will remember that the pauses occupied most of it. But even the artistes were staggered by the results. We whipped through the play and cut just the twenty minutes out of the play that night, and it was, I think, My Most Enjoyable Evening In the Theatre. It was, oddly enough, the only performance that seemed to go remotely well in Blackpool and, needless to say, we were on the verge of maniacal laughter throughout. Pozzo and his slave made every entrance and exit as if they were Belita and Chataway at the height of their powers, and after their disappearance in the first act one tramp had to comment in the course of the play:

'Well, that passed the time.'

'It would have passed in any case,' is the reply.

'Yes, but not quite so rapidly,' says the first tramp, which on this occasion was said with such meaning that they both started to go off into paroxysms, only stopped by the Messrs Bateson and Bull making threatening gestures from the wings.

We had a car waiting for us and, with most of our make-up still on, tore through the night only to find that we had ten minutes to spare at Preston station.

After this, the Pavilion Theatre, Bournemouth, was the Department of Anti-Climax, and we sent most of the inhabitants off into a deep sleep. Very comfortable seats and the sea air took away all the unpleasantness and, as usual, I stayed at the Seamoor Commercial Hotel and Café (prop. J. Gourlay) which costs, or did, under four pounds all in for actors. The Gourlays are sweet and kind, and, though there was a permanent TV show through the supper (until mercifully kibitzered by Mr Bateson's naughty feet getting entangled in the wires), it was also what is known as A Good Pull-Up for Carmen, which meant that one had a CHOICE in the evenings, which made a splendid change from ordinary digs where the plate is plonked in front of you william-nilliam. Also we had the use of their bathing-hut, which helped us through the week, during which we jolly nearly touched four figures.

Then gently down the coast to Brighton, where we were back to banging of seats and a certain amount of confusion. There was a night when a retired military gent could be heard inexplicably shouting above the turmoil: 'No wonder we lose the colonies if they put on drivel like this,' but we passed the £1,000 mark and the Headmaster of Lancing liked it (or so he said).

The next two weeks we were to play in the suburban theatres of London. It was delightful living at home again, and this comfort easily compensated for the appalling business we did at the gigantic Streatham Hill Theatre, where they threw pennies at the stage on the first night, but never into the box-office during the week. It was nice to move on to Golders Green the following week, where people seemed to enjoy the play for a change, and I had a dressing-room with a star on the door. This week we all started speaking to each other again, after losing our heads to such an extent in the purlieus of Streatham that notes were being left at the stage door.

Our lady patron, Miss Winifred Atwell, came to the matinée at Golders Green and seemed delighted with her property, though she carped a bit at the interval music. She thought it would be more in keeping with the mood of the piece to play some serious stuff (Schubert's 'Valse Triste' was a suggestion), but I did point out that the audience at most suburban and provincial theatres, to say nothing of the orchestras concerned, would leave in a body if *The Desert Song* and *The Student Prince* didn't pop up in the repertoire at least once a month.

I gave in my notice at Golders Green, but said I would play the extra week at Birmingham which had been tacked on to the end of the tour by this time. We were all beginning to feel the strain by now, and even Robert Eddison said he could not go on for more than a week after we all left. We played at the Birmingham Repertory Theatre, which is a charming bandbox of a theatre and I would love to be there in happier circs. There is also a table-tennis set in the wardrobe which makes it perfect. The resident company were away on a foreign tour and we were to fill the gap for two weeks. The booking was tremendous (the theatre only held about 600) and we were listened to in reverence and fairly stunned silence. In a way it was almost more maddening than hate and interruptions, but I was by now in a psychological state about the whole thing. We all found ourselves unable to speak to each other much off the stage, and the words came out automatically with even less meaning than they had had originally. I found the fortnight lying very heavily on my hands and could not wait for the final night of all.

Timothy and I caught the night train out of Birmingham, after having enjoyed one of the most expensive but happy dinners imaginable. It was 28 July 1956, a year almost to the day since we had started at the Arts. We felt so relaxed and relieved that we could only smile stupidly at each other as we bundled out in the dawn of Euston Station. Yet although we were able to throw off the physical side of *Waiting for Godot*, in my case certainly it was to haunt my memory for many a long month, as indeed Mr Hobson had prophesied.

In a casual assessment I would say that being in it did me far more good than any other performance I have ever given, and only a few weeks ago I was asked to do a Shell-Mex advertising film for TV and use my *Godot* voice, whatever that meant. I was asked to speak on the play to the British Drama League, an invitation which I fear they regretted, owing to the subsequent gibberish that poured out of my mouth.

I hadn't been back a week before dear Mr Donald Albery, who must have watched our meanderings round with the keenest enjoyment, was on the blower asking my reactions to a six weeks' season at the Comedy Theatre to lure the American tourists. I said that I would want £1,000 a week and two TRAINED nurses in attendance, and he didn't seem to think it was worth all THAT.

And although this is the end of that particular little section of my life, I have a lurking suspicion way back in my noddle that I shall end my days playing Pozzo in some of the less accessible repertory theatres of England. But heaven and the theatre-goers of Britain forbid!

8
On Being Remaindered

Only this week I got a letter from my publishers, asking me if I minded them remaindering my second book, *Bulls in the Meadows*.

Of course I didn't *mind*, I said, go ahead and see if I care. Then they asked me how many I wanted at 2s. 6d. a copy and then I was embarrassed and ordered eight and now I can't think who on earth I can give them to, as everyone who wanted to read the damned thing did so years ago. It's never been one of my favourite tomes, though the cover by Michael Gough is very pretty indeed and there is a picture inside of my mother with a grizzly bear on a lead, which is riveting in its way and well worth 2s. 6d. What will happen, I suppose, is that the book will pop up on all the bookstalls of the lesser-known London railway stations and my only hope is that some careless traveller, almost late for his train but desperately in need of literature, will grab *Bulls in the Meadows* and, if he's an aficionado, will think that it's about bull-fighting and hey presto there's another copy sold. Not that I get a farthing.

I would like to dispel immediately the theory that a writer makes a fortune out of writing. W.S. Maugham, N. Shute and I. Fleming did pretty well in their heyday, I've been told, but they must have been very much better at it than I. A few weeks ago I did receive a postal order for one shilling and sixpence, which (it said on the piece of paper that accompanied it) represented six months' earnings from my novel, *Not on Your Telly!* I have kept the postal order as a curiosity. Actually, to tell you the honest truth, it was rather a common book.

But the whole of my literary career has been fairly bizarre, and at the risk of your throwing this partic. vol. straight back at the public library from which you have borrowed it ('I never buy New Books' quote unquote the whole of the British Reading Public) I will retrace my Penguin's Progress. Its erratic lifeline does at least prove, as E.M. Forster says in *A Room with a View*, that Good Things can come out of a Muddle.

The 'muddle' I was in at its outset was getting the sack from the Shakespearian Company at Stratford-on-Avon and I retired, slightly hurt, to a friend's apartment, which he wasn't using at the time. I got in quite a good deal of cheese, some Alka-Seltzer and embarked on some Naval Reminiscences. I suppose at the back of my mind I had a fantasy that someone might be induced to publish them, but in fact I wanted to set down in black and white the things that happened to me during the war before I forgot them. I also wanted to pay a private and sentimental tribute to the crew of the ship which I had commanded for a great deal of the war.

Well, I finished it and bored the daylights out of most of my friends by reading them extracts. None of them suggested, however, that a publisher would leap at the chance of publishing it, until Alec Guinness, with whom I'd served as a sailor on and off through the war, said he'd show it to a friend of his who was one, I mean a publisher not a sailor. It was returned with regret but kindly comment and, emboldened by Alec's genuine enthusiasm, I started whizzing 'my work' round to every publisher whose address I could find. Finally it got stuck with a famous firm and remained there for a year. I was told that it was useless to try and hurry 'them' up and eventually I got it back with a polite but discouraging note. It wasn't meant to be discouraging but it was. Rationing of paper and the priority of more important books were mentioned among others as reasons for its rejection.

I put *I Mustn't Go Down to the Sea Again* (for that was the title of the book in those days) in the boot cupboard of my basement flat in Wellington Square, London SW3 and forgot all about it for a year or so. There was only one copy in a heavy black folder, typed by me and never, it must be admitted, in absolutely peak condition. I went on with my usual employment, viz. acting in my desultory way.

One day my friend and author (proper) Sewell Stokes asked me what had happened to 'that naval book of yours you're always banging on about'. I replied that as far as I knew it was in the boot cupboard of 'Sordid Hall', my Chelsea residence. Why? Because, said Sewell, I was in seeing My Publishers yesterday and They were saying that They had done very well out of a naval book about a submarine and were looking around for Another One. They were called Peter Davies Ltd and lived in Bedford Square. I dusted off the cover of my forgotten masterpiece and deposited it in their offices in the West Central One area, thinking in my heart of hearts: 'There goes my sole copy for another year or two.'

Not a bit of it. Within a matter of weeks I was summoned by the brothers Davies. They were called Peter and Nicholas and were very droll indeed. They looked at me gravely from across an imposing table.

'We like your book. It's very funny. We should like to publish it.'

I was overjoyed and started to stammer my thanks.

'But,' said Peter, 'might we ask what has happened to pages 81 and 82?'

I took a quick look at the pieces of paper he handed me. They had been almost entirely eaten away by mice, who seemed to have been intensely moved by my chapter on the Anzio beach-head.

I assured them that I could remedy this defect in my work and they said they'd give me twenty-five pounds there and then and a further twenty-five pounds on the day of publication.

Now, though I was by this time receiving fifty pounds and upwards for one day's film work, I can only tell you that I went out into the summer sunshine and rode back on air on the top of a 19 bus.

The subsequent waiting period appeared to be interminable, though goodness knows there was lots to do. To begin with there were the proofs to be corrected. This is, I think, the most boring job in the world. I find my attention wandering the whole time and miss the most obvious mistakes. The silly part of it all is that one of the only things I ever learned during my short time as a journalist was proof-correcting, and that was *before* I became a proper writer. I had to use all those hieroglyphics when I was sub-sub-sub editor on the *Graphic*. Nowadays I have a kind friend called John Grant, who corrects my proofs out of I don't know what. It must be chivalry; at any rate I can never repay the debt. He even leaves in the deliberate mistakes I make which is super.

Then there was the question of the cover. The Davies Brothers were quite keen on my idea of Roger Furse as designer, as one of them had been at school with him. He was my art director before the war at the Summer Theatre in Perranporth and had been my commanding officer for a short time during it so it all Fitted In, as my dear mother would have said. He did a strikingly patriotic drawing with a lot of blue and red which I think helped the book along quite a bit. It in no way resembled the front of the paperback version, which appeared some years later and was, I thought, dreamy. It showed what must have been meant to be me, looking strikingly like the late dear Tyrone Power, in a steel helmet undergoing the most frightful personal bombardment.

But the greatest problem was the title. The Davieses thought *I Mustn't Go Down to the Sea Again* a bit cumbersome and I suppose they were right. The same criticism applied to *The Lieut-Commander Hates the Sea* which was also a tidge reminiscent. I waited for inspiration. It didn't come. Not to me at any rate. I was sitting gloomily with my friend, Maurice Kaufmann, actor, bon viveur and footballer, when he suddenly said 'To Sea in a Sieve' out of the blue. One knew that it was the Only Title the moment he opened his trap. The ships I served in were all sieves and did indeed all go to sea. Simple as that. Unfortunately since then Mr K. has relapsed into silence whenever I ask him for further assistance in this particular field. But maybe the Oracle will speak again one day: or indeed the Oracle's wife, Miss H. Blackman.

After all this dodgy stuff there was nothing one could do except wait for the Advance Copies. The moment of their arrival provided the most thrilling moment in my life. They smelt so lovely for one thing, and they said in print that I'd written something that was going to cost fifteen shillings to buy. It was staggering. But I couldn't honestly picture the sort of person who was going to go into a bookshop and plonk down his or her moolah for *To Sea in a Sieve*. I walked about in a daze, waiting for Publication Day, not helped by the fact that I was still appearing in *Waiting for Godot*.

The volume was published on Tuesday 28 February 1956. I got a jolly good write-up in the *Sunday Times* two days before and a long interview in the *Daily Herald* on the actual date. Can't quite remember how I behaved that Tuesday though the Furses, Maurice the Title-Finder and I drank a bit of champagne and in the post-meridiem I felt a little flat and beetled up to the offices of Peter Davies the Publishers to collect the remaining twenty-five pounds due to me on the day of publication. Although I understood only too clearly that this sum was in advance of royalties (and it was pointed out to me that these might never even amount to the fifty pounds) I thought it might be satisfying just to hold a little actual money in my hot hand.

In Bedford Square the Davies brothers were a trifle cagey, I thought. Nice, but cagey, and one of them did tell me that as I had had free copies of my book (at 10s a head Trade Price) sent to most of my crew, there was nothing left of the £25. I thought at any moment they might ask *me* for money, so I hurried off, crestfallen.

The next morning I was opening my mail casually and suddenly a cheque fluttered to the ground. It was for well over £400 and was from Peter Davies Ltd. I went into the loo and threw up. I thought it must be a mistake or a joke in the worst possible taste. I read the letter which swam in front of my eyes. The phrase that has stuck in my mind ever since was '8,000 sold before publication'. And that's what this astonishing document had written on it. It took some digesting, I don't mind telling you.

'But how,' I reasoned, 'could 8,000 obviously unbalanced people have been fooled into buying *To Sea in a Sieve* before even reading the reviews?'

What I didn't know then was that, if the Messrs Smith and Boot liked something they had got hold of before publication, they would then buy literally thousands of copies for both their library and retail departments. I found I was a Boots Book of the Month, which, believe you me, is a highly satisfactory thing to be. I went round singing 'I'm one of the Bootses Books of the Month', to the tune of 'Barcelona', which perplexed some of the passers-by, but Chelsea folk are v. sophisticated and soon got used to it. The local bookshops gave me magnificent displays in their windows and I got severely above myself.

It was pretty heady stuff as far as I was concerned and I was already way out in a dream world of my own invention.

'Now I can at last give up acting,' I said to myself as a reprint was ordered. As the first printing had consisted of 15,000 and the reprint was another 3,500 I was almost in the Best Seller class, which is apparently technically anything above 17,000 hardbacks (as the dears are called). I found I was being wined, dined and even teaed by film moguls. I didn't unfortunately see the writing on the wall and the best offer, after a good deal of parleying, seemed to hover around £250 for a six-month option, which appeared ludicrously little to me. Some of the tycoons had spent nearly that sum on giving me a few lunches. But the time was slipping by and even I, inexperienced as I was, realized that the book would be as dead as mutton in six months. A great many more sea books would have appeared and the taste might suddenly change overnight. The luck originally had been in the timing. The public was getting a little tired of the fantastically realistic but serious destroyer, cruiser and submarine epics and my frivolous tome about the ineptitude and curious situations that landing craft were prone to made a contrast. The fact that publishers had turned it down two years back was in fact a blessing in disguise for me.

But the dream of a fortune out of the film rights came straight out of my pipe and retreated up there again. By a series of curious misunderstandings I managed to sell the thing to Romulus Films (the Woolf Brothers) for £1,500 outright. It was bought apparently as a vehicle for Kenneth More, who didn't fancy the idea, and in fact the film has never been made. I'm not remotely surprised, as, apart from the title, there seems no value there or anything which could pass for a story. But on the other hand one never knows in our bizarre profession. I remember being rung up in the middle of the night by an American TV tycoon who wanted to buy *To Sea in a Sieve* as a TV 'spectacular'.

'But yes,' I cried, still half asleep and unable to believe my ears.

'In that case,' he continued, 'as you are a great friend of Alec Guinness's, couldn't you persuade him to play you?'

'No,' I said sharply.

'Well, what about Robert Morley?'

I rang off and went back to sleep.

I told Alec later. 'Why didn't you say yes?' he said. 'And then you could have played me.' I have to point out, in my usual book-dropping way that Sir Alec featured in the book as we used to get tied up together quite often, our ships I mean.

Apart from the sale of the film rights, the other surprise for me of the New World I was entering was something known as A Signing Session.

Have you ever attended a signing session? It's quite an experience. At the time when the subject was brought up by the Davies Brothers, I was so giddy from the excitement of it all, that I was clay in their mitts. I clapped them and readily assented, thinking it was probably a game for proper authors.

I was to carry out the operations at two of the Metropolisses (oh dear, that looks wrong for a start!) stores of repute, viz. the Army and Navy Stores and Hatchards. Apparently all I had to do was sit in a cosy armchair, surrounded by copies of *To Sea in a Sieve*. I was instructed to smile continuously and dish them out to the eager customers as quickly and charmingly as possible. It would appear to be a very easy way of making money, as apart from the wear and tear to my pen (2s. 9d. from Boots the Cash Chemists) it should work out at 1s. 5d. per copy to me. It seemed that I simply could not go wrong.

The day of my first assignment dawned bright and clear, and fortified by a glass of sherry-wine provided by Edward Addison of the promotion dept of P. Davies, I hied myself to the dear old Army and Navy Stores. I took a lift to the book department, to spare myself undue exertion, and after a cursory look at the Sensible Tweed counters, which seemed to have gone berserk, I located Books. It was the lunch hour and the area was full of what looked to me prospective, if hungry, buyers of *To Sea in a Sieve*.

I was led to a table and given a steel chair, a blotting-pad and a rather curious look by a serious lady in a print dress. There were about 482 copies of my book littering the table and environs. I sat down nervously but with a kind of exhilaration and extracted my pen from its hiding-place. I looked around expectantly and, though there were plenty of people about, no one was remotely fascinated by my presence. I saw no way to make it Felt. I tried to twiddle my ballpoint nonchalantly.

Twenty minutes later my first client appeared. Well not really a client, it was Peter Woodthorpe, one of the tramps in *Godot*. He carried a brown paper parcel in his hand and a bit of a smirk on his face. Silently he withdrew the contents of the former and furtively opened it on the inside cover. I signed it affectionately and with a flourish but instinct made me examine the book carefully. It was *Bull Fever* by Kenneth Tynan. I realized it was a Joke. I chased Mr Woodthorpe through the Silverware Dept and gloomily resumed what can only be described as my crouching position. A lot of ladies and gentlemen had at long last become interested in my movements, stared in blank amazement and, when I tried to meet their gaze unflinchingly, turned away to the paperbacks. I put my head in my hands and moaned quietly to myself.

A few minutes later, a kind saleslady, obviously thinking I was about to end it all by jumping out of the window of the jolly old A and S stores, brought a dozen copies of *To Sea in a Sieve* to my table, making about 494 in all. She asked me to sign these please as they were 'telephone orders'. This statement was gibberish to me until she explained that the store had taken space in the Personal Columns of both *The Times* and the *Telegraph* and had informed patrons that they needn't attend the signing session in person (like me) but could phone for an autographed copy. On second or third thoughts I realized that 14s. in the hand was better than a slap in the belly with a wet fish, as my dear old piano-teacher used to say.

After this rewarding little interlude there was a further lull broken by Mr Addison (promotion). He asked me if I realized that

Richard Todd, the star of the film, had sold very few copies of *The Dam Busters* at a Signing Session in Bentalls at Kingston-on-Thames. I replied sourly that *that* had nothing to do with anything.

I was beginning to get very restive. I wandered round the department, looking at Other People's books, but ready to do a lightning sprint back to my table at the first sign of life. But I needn't have bothered. I was ploughing through a book about someone called Ulysses, who on closer inspection seemed to have very little to do with the Greek gent of that name, when I was told that the S.S. was over, thank you very much, Mr Bull. I slunk into the restaurant, where for further self-mortification I chose Toad in the Hole.

It was too late to get out of my second Signing Session, but Forewarned is Forearmed as I think my grandmother used to say. Well, someone used to say it. I planned to forestall (that's three fores in a row which should make a Round Dozen but doesn't) total humiliation in Hatchards, my next pillory, by bribing my friends into lending their support. Their duties were quite clear. In return for the Highest Tea, to be served at Fortnum and Masons no less, they were to tear into Hatchards at a given moment, form an Admiring Crowd round me and beg me to sign copies of *To Sea in a Sieve*. These, to be provided by me, they would have concealed about their persons.

But my plans went sadly agley. (No, not ugly, you fools, agley, agley, agley, from Scot. gley, squint.)

To begin with, there was an air of intense claustrophobia in the store and, though it is much smarter and bookier than the dear old Army and Navy emporium, it is much smaller. I also had a slight shock when I came face to face with the table where I was to sit. There were again hundreds of copies of the book, but this time crowned by an immense and repulsive cardboard cut-out of me as Pozzo in *Waiting for Godot*.

It really wasn't very attractive, though it might have formed the basis for a weapon if open warfare was declared, but I could not think it inspired confidence in the cash customers. There was just a faint hope that some of them might guess that *To Sea in a Sieve* was something to do with the History of Naval Punishment (cats o'nine tails and all that caper) because the picture showed me carrying a whip, but it was a v. off chance. I decided that the only thing to do was to hide myself as best as I could and every now and again peer out behind what I thought was an ingratiating and enchanting smile. I was told later by kind friends that it registered as a lecherous leer, which, I suppose, accounts for some of the horrified looks I glimpsed.

However, it must be confessed that actual business was a distinct improvement on the previous débâcle, and I did sell two copies for strict cash. I can only put it down to the fact that the percentage of mentally unbalanced 'passing trade' in Piccadilly is higher than that in Victoria Street. One purchaser was a gent who said he'd served under me in the war, and could not have been a day under eighty. I had never seen him before in all my puff. The other was a dear old lady who liked the cover but told me confidentially that it was doubtful if she would be able to find time to read the book.

Morale rose, and reached fever-pitch when a distinguished-looking gentleman approached me with a very smart lady indeed.

'I'm the Duke of Blankshire,' he said extending his hand, 'and this' – he paused for effect – 'is Mrs Entwhistle.'

This was a conversation stopper as far as I was concerned as I've always had trouble with words like Entwhistle, quite apart from anything else. I smiled benignly and said nothing. His Grace helped me out of the *impasse*.

'Two copies please,' he said. 'One for me and one – for Mrs Entwhistle.'

He indicated her with a broad sweep of the arm which struck her, about sixty copies of *To Sea in a Sieve* and the cardboard cut-out of me in *Waiting for G*. All the immediately attacked fell to the ground. I picked Mrs Entwhistle up (it seemed the least I could do) and joined the Duke on the floor, where we must have looked as if we were Playing Bears. It wasn't quite the moment I would have chosen myself for my friends to come rushing into the shop as if escaping from a tidal wave which had engulfed Swan and Edgars. But they did and hysteria swept the building.

After what seemed hours later we adjourned to jolly old Fortnum and Masons where my so-called friends went through the bill of fare like locusts and I found that the 5s. 8d. that I had earned during the afternoon did not quite cover the bill.

My second effort was the now being remaindered tome, *Bulls in the Meadows*. Writing it was a pretty big headache and I would give this piece of gratuitous advice to intending biographers: 'Never write about your family while they are still living.'

Dearly as I love my brothers, and I hope vice versa, the proposed book nearly provided a lasting rift. Memories of our childhood days, which appeared excruciatingly funny and innocuous to me, were deemed bad taste and unsuitable for public consumption by them. When I had completed the vol. I gave a copy to each of them and one to my mother. I called on the latter first to ascertain her reactions and if she wanted me to make any excisions or amendments.

'Only two,' she said. 'I changed from petticoats to knickers in 1911 not 1910, and I'm a rising eighty-seven not eight-eight.'

I pointed out to her gently that by the time the book eventually appeared she would be a rising eighty-eight.

'Oh,' she said, 'then that's all right but I'm afraid you're going to have a bit of trouble with the boys.' Up till the day of her death she was still referring to us as 'the boys' though we were all a rising fifty something.

'The Boys' were actually absolutely justified in making a fuss as it had been our father's express wish that anything he had written down in either his or our diaries must not be published if it was likely to cause anyone embarrassment or distress. So what with the laws of libel and so many lawyers' secrets being contained in the material at hand, I had to go very carefully indeed. Sometimes I despaired of getting any continuity at all and in my opinion the finished and emasculated book was a trifle dull. On the other hand it achieved its dual object. I had always wanted to write about my father, whom I'd loved and admired, and I had wanted if possible to get the book published in my mother's lifetime.

Bulls in the Meadows came out roughly eighteen months after my literary début. Its appearance luckily coincided with my taking part in the Edinburgh Festival in a disasterette entitled *Man of Distinction*. I say 'luckily' because it at least meant that there was a publicity tie-up to the strings of my rather wobbly bow. Not that I embarked on a new series of Signing Sessions but I did carry on like a banshee in Ladies' Clubs and in and out of TV and radio magazine programmes. The book got on the whole very good reviews (super ones in the *Sunday Times* (Valentine Heywood) and the *Evening News* (John Connell) and a stinker from Muriel Spark somewhere). It sold just about 5,500 copies and earned me £350 and brought me to my senses with a bump. This is the financial point. I believe (although I was told this a few years back) that publishers can make a profit on any book which sells 3,000 or more, so I suppose I cannot complain but it doesn't make for a feeling of security to stick around the 5,000 to 6,000 mark, which I seem to do regularly. I don't think I can describe myself as that 'increasingly popular literary figure' do you?

But in spite of the disappointment caused by my second book, my first was having a second lease of life. We managed (or rather clever P. Davies did) to do a double sell of *To Sea in a Sieve* to Odhams Press, by which they printed it first in a condensed version with several other works and then in Panther Books at 2s. 6d. a copy. The latter (30,000 copies) disappeared within a few weeks and for reasons I can't fathom was never reprinted. I got about a farthing a copy out of it and it added up to quite a jolly little sum, which is more than the French version did.

This was entitled *En Mer dans une Passoir* (no, dear, not *Pissoir*) and was translated by a jolly French lady who must have found my English murder. There are a series of wonderful footnotes one of which reads, *'Ivor Novello fut longtemps considéré comme un rival de Noel Coward.'* It really looks very handsome indeed in a green and white paper cover and disappeared as quickly and silently as it arrived. I've never had any statement from anybody. We got fifty quid for the rights (P. Davies and I) and as far as I know that sum was never reached in royalties unless Editions Gallimards are being filthy cheats, which I know is *incroyable.*

Anyhow there were now three of My Books on my shelves, counting the Frog one, and I thought I'd better press on. I decided to have a bash at theatrical reminiscences. It was obviously no good writing about anyone else except myself as I was unlikely to object to anything I wrote about me.

The book was called *I Know the Face, but . . .* and I really enjoyed writing that one. It caused a mild flutter and a great many people seemed to read a great many other people's copies, because I again made every bit of £350 (5,000 vols about). Everyone was super about it critically. Mr Harold Hobson devoted space to it in his theatre columns, which, with a book review in the same paper, is about as perfect a combination as one could desire, let's face it.

Mr Kenneth Tynan mentioned it in the *New Yorker* which I thought would ensure a flood of offers from American publishers. Not a sausage! Even when I went over there and tried to flog all my wares, the books might just as well have been treatises on the treatment and cure of halitosis in Hindustani for all the interest displayed. It just seems as if I am incapable of actually making money out of My Writing. Not that I'm grumbling, as I keep on trying to tell you. Well, not grumbling much. No, seriously, I've always had the breaks and I am not so silly as not to know that. But it's becoming increasingly obvious that I'm not for general consumption, but have a specialized appeal. I made a mild bid for the General Public, whoever they are, with a novel called *Not on Your Telly!* I thought it was about time I stopped talking about myself but, as my friends hastened to point out, I was easily identified with most of the characters in it, both male and female. I must admit that all my dialogue is readily interchangeable, sex-wise, but isn't that just Life?

I registered the two panel games I invented for the book, namely 'What's the Smell?' and 'Beat the Death-Watch Beetle' thinking quite loonily that some enterprising TV producer might seriously think they were possible for Real. But no! The only offshoot of *Not on Your Telly!* was an offer to write a pilot for a TV series starring that well-known and pretty Miss Shirley Abicair, who plays the zither so successfully. But this idea didn't seem frightfully practical so I retired with the usual sum in my hands. Luckily the money I get in advance has increased, though it all comes to the same thing in the end. And what is that, you ask?

Being remaindered or running the risk of same.

9
Luther

It all began oddly enough in the then tiny fishing-village of Fuengirola on the Costa da Sol in Spain. A script was brought to me on the beach in a large envelope by the postman, which was the kind of service you used to get around those parts before they were invaded by tourists, rich land-buying prospectors of every nationality, the Duke and Duchess of Windsor, and one or two ladies who used to be gentlemen and vice versa. Now even in Fuengirola there is a self-service store and an ice-cream parlour which offers twelve flavours. Actually I don't mind that so much.

Well, in the envelope there was this new play of John Osborne's and very classy reading it made. On the other hand the sender(s) did not mention what part they had me in mind for and, without being too conceited I hope, there were at least five I could have had a bash at. An additional snag from my point of view was that the play was to be presented by the English Stage Company who were being *avant-garde* at the time in the Royal Court Theatre above Sloane Square Station. I had been alarmed by the rumours of mime and movement classes, and talks on the Theory of Acting. My opinion about the latter corresponds roughly to that purported to have been expounded by Miss Pamela Brown, when asked by an interviewer in New York if she had any words of advice to the young aspirant for stage honours:

'Yes,' said Miss Brown, 'get on, say the wordies loud and clear, and get off.'

On the other hand I did realize that I hadn't been in what we actors snobbily call a 'prestige' play since jolly old *Godot* and in a purely masochistic way felt impelled to have another 'go' at the stage proper. I had left the country for Spain after appearing with my beloved friend, Mr R. Morley, in a television series called *If the Crown Fits*, which, to put it mildly, hadn't exactly set the aerials allocated to Associated Television on fire. Although it was shown at a peak time of a Saturday night, the click of sets turning over to Auntie BBC was deafening, after the first episode had been viewed. Even Mr Morley said to me afterwards, with a pained expression on his dear face:

'They really *hated* it, Bully.'

And it was true, for months later, when on tour with *Luther* I would be out with John Moffatt in some provincial town and we would see someone staring at me in a particularly hostile way. Mr M. would grab me by the arm and drag me up some side street hissing, 'Cave. She had an *If the Crown Fits* face on.'

Anyhow, while still in Spain I got a note from the English Stage Coy, saying would I now read the play quote 'with a view' unquote to being considered for the part of Tetzel, the wicked old seller of Papal Indulgences. Now this is a quite marvellous role in my opinion and superbly written. But, and it was a big 'but' for me, it had one long speech lasting about eight minutes and I have a phobia about long speeches. Even considering 'being considered' therefore represented to me considerably more than what Sir John Gielgud calls 'A Challenge'. After a week of self-torture, I sent the play back via my agent with a polite note of negation. Shortly afterwards I returned to London and got involved in a series of other projects, including a major television play and a minor quota unquota film. Suddenly out of the blue, or rather from the other end of the King's Road, Chelsea, there came a firm offer to play Tetzel in *Luther*. As it was only a few days from the actual starting date of rehearsals, it was clear that they had reached the bottom of the barrel. The script came whizzing round again, I took another peek at it, got acute stage fright immediately and called up Miss Doreen Dixon, the casting director, to say 'No' yet again, and I added that I would bring the script back later that afternoon, as it was in brisk demand.

I was fraught with doubt and a sort of nagging regret because since my return to the capital I had been having constant intercourse on the phone with John Moffatt, who had already been engaged for *Luther* to play Cardinal Cajetan. He had tried to talk me into joining him by bribing me with the thought of the huge tucks-in we would enjoy during the proposed continental tour of the play. For *Luther* was bound not only for the Paris Festival but a Dutch one as well. However my innate terror had seized me by the throat again and in a sort of coma of relief I started to study the script of the TV play to which I was already committed.

The telephone bell went and I was informed that Mr Tony Richardson wanted to speak to me. As the director of *Luther* was about the last person I wanted to speak to at that moment, I should have put the receiver down and rushed out of the building. I did say 'No' when he asked me to come and discuss the play. No, thank you very much indeed, I said. Would I return the script to him then at the Royal Court Hotel Bar and just have a drink? He'd always wanted to meet me, he said.

I tried to be cool, calm and collected a few hours later, sipping a Campari. The conversation was so racy that I lost all control. It went something like this, I think:

'Gracious you *are* sunburned,' said Mr Richardson.

'I suppose I am.'

'Where did you get it?'

'Fuengirola.'

'How are things at the lodging-house of the Central?' asked Mr Richardson.

As 'Los Huespedes Del Centro' is about the most remote and Spanish of all the Pensiones in that part of the world, I couldn't imagine Mr Richardson there with all those hens and pigs, who tend to roam about at whim. But there he had stayed some years previously, and now after regaling me with some splendid gossip about the local inhabs I seemed to be playing Tetzel in *Luther* about a quarter of an hour later.

Afterwards he asked me why I had changed my mind and when I gave my two reasons, he thought they were the most bizarre he had ever heard for accepting a role. I said I was only doing it because it promised untold games of Scrabble and eating orgies with my friend John Moffatt. It was not the sort of thing that should have gone down wildly well with one of the directors of the English Stage Company but it did. As I learned afterwards, Tony is such a unique and astute person that he can change his whole attitude, chameleon-like, to suit the person with whom he's dealing.

The first reading of *Luther* was alarming enough, in all conscience. The only thing that could be said in its favour was that it was held at a public house called the Six Bells which is every bit of 200 yards away from my residence. A lot of the rehearsals were to be held there which was Handy, not that I was asked to attend many. Apart from a brief scene with John Moffat and Albert Finney, I was only required for what came to be known as the 'Tetzel scene', which sounds rather grand. But indeed it could hardly be described as anything else, as no other person, except the audience occasion-ally, was allowed to get a word in edgeways.

Anyhow, the first reading went through without Incident. It didn't however follow the pattern of most of the FRs I have attended. Usually the cast tends (a) to wear their best clothes and (b) to hold back with the acting to such an extent that it is almost impossible to hear the words of the play on which one is embarking. The probable explanation of the latter is that the average actor has so little self-confidence that he (or she) doesn't dare risk getting the sack on the first day by an over-enthusiastic display of histrionics. Which reminds me of that delightful story of the famous star being encouraged by a tentative director during the first week of rehearsals:

'Ah Miss X,' he said. 'It's coming along nicely.'

'*Coming along?*' exploded the star. '*Coming along? That's it.*'

At the Six Bells on the afternoon in question everything seemed a bit topside-turvey to me. Most of the company looked as if they'd just returned from a juicy day's pot-holing and this, I have to report, went for the Herr Direktor and the star, Mr A. Finney. And it was clear from the start that neither Mr F. nor Mr Bill Owen, who was playing Luther Senior, were Holding Back. In fact they were both using such voice that I was amazed that we didn't have the whole of the staff of the Chelsea Foot Clinic from opposite running over in horror to see what in the world was happening.

I sat there frozen to my chair and by the time we came to my bit (at the beginning of the second act), I had decided there was nothing to do but Let Fly. This I did and suspect that I was never quite so good ever again. After an encouraging smile from Mr Moffatt I sat back shaking like a v. large leaf.

Mr Richardson was more than generous after this exhibition and I managed to walk home the 200 yards unattended. I was not called on again to practise for over a week and by the end of this period I'd worried myself practically out of the play and was writing letters of resignation. How tiresome can one get, for goodness' sake? Answer: Intolerably! Right! It was all senseless because by this time I knew the words backwards but nothing would convince me that they would come out frontwards from my mouth on the opening night. Mr Osborne, as far as I know, kept away from most of the rehearsals, though I quite suddenly got a super note of encouragement after a run-through in a darkened Saville Theatre. But he was, and is, a pretty ideal playwright from an actor's point of view, as having been one himself for a long time, he knows exactly what to say, when to say it and how.

We were scheduled to open at Nottingham on 26 June and a few days before we left London Princess Margaret and Lord Snowdon popped into the Royal Court to see a run through. Haven't done much name-dropping recently and this sort of book Needs it. I don't think they enjoyed it frightfully but they did see it naked without the sets or most of the costumes. And visually *Luther* owed a tremendous debt to Jocelyn Herbert's décor, which was deeply impressive. And one of the most remarkable things about it was that, though it was designed primarily for the tiny Royal Court Theatre, it looked equally splendid in the vast Opera House, Manchester, to say nothing of the Sarah Bernhardt Théâtre in Paris.

We journeyed to Nottingham on the Sunday before opening and Jimmy Cairncross (The Prior and Chancellor Eck), John Moffatt and I stayed in a not wildly satisfactory hotel in Clumber Street. Clean and quiet but no full board. And heaven knows Mr M. and I like Full Board and the Fuller the better.

Owing to stage complications we didn't get round to a proper dress rehearsal till quite late on the Monday, when we were opening. It was of course during a heat wave (it always is when a costume play is born) and it seemed impossible to breathe in the theatre. Johnny Moff and I went on a Lucozade Jag and consumed bott. after bott. to give us energy. All we appeared to get was a great deal of wind and not of the cooling kind. It was a tetchy time. One of the hawks or falcons engaged for the production flew away from Tony Richardson's arm and the understudy had to go on.

'Poor little bird wants to have a bit of a fly,' said Mr Richardson and that was the last we saw of it.

The first night was an ordeal for all concerned, including I think many of the audience, who had to leave before the end to catch their buses home or risk having to walk. The waits between scenes seemed interminable and the play lasted four and a quarter hours on this particular occasion. But though it was to be cut considerably, it never played under the full three hours. Most of us thought that this playing time (the first act was an hour exactly) would mitigate against its chances not only in London but later in New York. But in fact the reverse must have happened and its very length must have impressed the customers and cancelled out a usual box-office weakness.

But we were to run into difficulties at Nottingham later in the week. The usual custom at the Theatre Royal was to have a Wednesday performance at five o'clock in addition to the normal evening one. It was obvious that this would not quite be practical with *Luther*, as its length was inconsistent with the time allotted for entertainment in that area. The authorities decided, as the running time was still around the three and a half hour mark, to cut out the Cardinal Cajetan scene for a five o'clock perf. So I left him (the Cardinal) lying in the long grass in Nottingham's great park, while I went to sweat my guts out twice. When Mr Moffatt came into the theatre eventually he found a note lying on his dressing-room table. It read: 'Thought you were a bit down at the matinée.' It was signed A. Finney.

I wonder if this is the moment to go into a long diatribe on the

talent and character of this remarkable young man? Perhaps I'd
better press on as he hates that sort of thing. But remarkable Mr
Finney is, I don't mind telling you. I think I once described him as the
only unboring dedicated actor I know and this, combined with his
gift for friendship, makes him a pretty valuable person.

Well, having left Notts County we proceeded to the Théâtre des
Nations Festival at the Sarah Bernhardt Théâtre in Paris, France. It
was a great treat to play there, conditions-wise. Mr M. and I had a
dressing-room overlooking the Seine, with a lady dresser to go with
it. Mr Finney had the divine Sarah's own room, which looked as if
she'd just left it. Even her wig-blocks had remained on the table. The
whole theatre had an incredible atmosphere and the acoustics were
marvellous. The stage staff, as in the Dutch theatres subsequently,
were impeccable and really seemed to care about 'the theatre' which
is unheard of in most British and American playhouses. Here, on the
Continent, they walked about in plimsolls or carpet slippers,
listened and watched the play every night. They were also friendly,
courteous and interested. In most touring theatres in Britain the
heavier the hobnailed boots can thump, the louder the talk can be,
the more bedlam and din that can be raised during a scene change,
the happier and more important the average stage hand will feel.

The first performance in Paris went smoothly but, owing to the
proverbial unpunctuality of the Parisian audience, the curtain fell
long after midnight. The management had wisely not informed the
company that the English critics were attending the performance.
These included Mr Robert Morley, who loathed the play and went
round afterwards dropping bricks like confetti ('Such pretty scenery,'
he said to Miss Herbert, which is the one thing it wasn't). He ended
up in our room, snipping off my dressing-gown cord, in order to take
me out to supper. He made me a fairly eccentric bow-tie and we went
to a very smart restaurant in Montmartre, where there wasn't a tie to
be seen, owing to the heat-wave.

We played five performances in the French capital and Albert won
the award for the best performance of the Festival. The Messrs
Tynan and Hobson came out with rave notices in their Sunday
columns, which was a wonderful augury for London, as it would be

as difficult for them to retract as it was for dear old M. Luther.

Sunday was our last perf in Paris and the following day we travelled in a quite beautiful train to the Hague. We stayed at a curiously old-fashioned watering place called Scheveningen or something like that. The food was fabulous (three choices of cheese at least for brekker to start the day off with) and Mr Moffatt and I 'went ape', as an American chum of mine would put it. We were particularly entranced by the Balinese-type restaurant which used to serve just the twenty different dishes as a first-course. Mr Moffatt took some photographs of me at it in colour and vice versa and if they don't come under the heading of 'filthy pictures' I'd like to know what does.

We played and stuffed ourselves silly in the Hague, Rotterdam, Utrecht and Amsterdam and the audiences were fantastic. Ditto the stage staffs and ditto, perhaps above all, our stage management. We had the most incredible young lady called Jocelyn Tawse as our stage director. She was not only quite a dish but she was also the most efficient, respected *and* liked SD I have run across in my eighty years in the theatre.

I think our favourite Dutch date was Amsterdam. Quite apart from the (to me) unexpected great beauty of the city, the warmth of the audiences was amazing and they appeared to appreciate points which were to pass unnoticed in London and New York. The only people who didn't obviously enjoy the play were the British Ambassador and his immediate entourage. But HE did unwittingly hand us one of the big belly laughs of the tour. He kindly provided a gala supper at the Embassy and I arrived a bit later than the others. I was greeted by the first diplomat (British) in Holland, who had been chatting to the Messrs Devine, Finney and others.

'Ah, Mr Bull,' he said cordially as he greeted me, 'I have been waiting for you. You were the only one who spoke up tonight. I could *hear* you.'

I went purple in the face with embarrassment until I happened to notice that he was carrying a hearing aid. I whispered under my breath to those in breathshot that I'd tone down my perf a bit the next night. But for tact and diplomacy this sally seemed to take a good deal of beating, as luckily did the super supper, on which we fell like so many locusts.

We flew back regretfully to London and then to face the Department of Utter Anti-Climax, in Manchester, where we were back in the Kingdom (United) of missed lighting cues, stage hands having private rows so publicly that one could hardly hear oneself speak on the stage and practically nowhere to eat after the show within our pocket-range. Luckily Johnny Moff. and I were chez Mrs Leech, one of the last of the theatrical landladies in the Great Tradition. The awful thing is that she cannot have made a halfpenny out of us or indeed a great many of the hogs and hoggesses who haunted her precincts. She seemed intent on stuffing Mr M. and me to bursting point and she very nearly succeeded.

In the Opera House everything was swinging, apart from the stage hands who should have been. In the wardrobe a certain amount of adjustment had been necessary to the costumes, some of which had been stretched to ripping-point by dirty books, transistor radio sets and other dutiable goods from the 'continong the continong it is très bong so allez nous ong', as my father used to sing when we were children. Business was fantastic and I don't think it was entirely due to Local Boy (A. Finney, Salford-born) Making Good. The receptions at the end were wildly enthusiastic, the local television big-wigs and toupées were equally patronizing and we did around £6,000 on the week which broke quite a lot of records.

One of the strengths of *Luther* was the authentic and hypnotic atmosphere of the monastery ritual in the first act. This was greatly enhanced by the music, which was arranged and occasionally composed by John Addison (who did the same with *Tom Jones* a couple of years later). We had a number of very good singers, who disintegrated slowly towards the end of the run in London. They seemed to have some mysterious contract, by which, if they could find a 'substitute', they could beetle off and fulfil some more lucrative engagement. They could then return to the play if and when the fancy took them. It was at first unnerving to me to come on the stage at a matinée and find myself facing an entirely fresh set of monks, and yet I really cannot complain, as they inevitably coped perfectly competently with chants, props and exits, which I doubt they'd ever come across before that afternoon.

But the original Singing Monks did make the most beautiful noises and I didn't, I fear, realize their supreme importance to the entertainment until one day in Manchester. I was in Boots the Cash Chemists as usual, when a gent approached and asked if I was me, no, asked if I was I. I said I was I and he asked if he could accompany I down to the theatre, as he was going there. I said of course and he started to discuss the play. He was going to see it now for the second time, he told me, because on his first visit he hadn't been able to concentrate enough on the work of Andrew Pearman. My eyebrows shot up like hairy rockets. I knew that Andrew was one of the monks but this was the first time I'd heard his name singled out.

'Oh yes,' I said inanely, 'he's very good isn't he?'

'Good!' snorted my companion contemptuously. 'He's only about the finest counter-tenor in England!'

So that put me in my place. I listened very carefully to the singing at the next performance and was deeply impressed afresh by the beautiful sounds that Mr P., and indeed all the monks, were emitting.

Mr Moffatt and I left Manchester on the Saturday night train and made for our cosy nests with the usual window-box problems. We were due to open at the Royal Court later in the week but there were several public dress rehearsals, during which one had to get accustomed to the very limited accommodation back stage. Entrances and exits were extremely dodgy and there was hardly room to swing a cat, let alone Afghan hounds, falcons and thirty-odd actors.

The day of the first night was on us before we realized, and a very odd day it turned out to be. After a 'walk-through' in the afternoon the Messrs Finney, Cairncross and Moffatt came back to my flat as it was readily accessible to the theatre. A kind friend had given me a Rolls Royce as a first-night present. Well, not actually given it me. He had hired it for the day, as he thought it might make a change from the 19 and 22 buses. It did.

And so we all had a highish tea and Albert had a bad throat and in between stuffing himself disappeared under a bath towel to sniff some Friars Balsam (v. appropriate under the Lutheran circs) up his snitch. We all offered up silent prayers that his voice would hold out through the evening.

I was having a bit of trouble with my throat myself and I did a rather awful thing. I made a bargain with God, which is just what Martin Luther said you mustn't do. It was a frightfully one-sided selfish bargain too. 'If you'll get me through tonight,' I said, 'I'll give up smoking.' He did and I did. And I won't bang on about it any more because I tend to become smug and the whole thing is unattractive to the normal person, particularly if he or she is a smoker. People really get very cross when they offer me a cigarette and I say, 'No thank you, I gave it up on 28 July 1961.' You see I am quite incapable of saying just, 'No thanks,' or 'I don't smoke.'

Even though I was imbued with a certain amount of faith that evening, it was still pretty nerve-wracking. I had to make my first appearance on a cart. It was the most wonderful theatrical entrance one could wish for. I was preceded by a tatty band of singing monks and a couple of children banging cymbals. The only snag, owing to the confined space at the Royal Court, was the manoeuvring of the cart on to the stage and, in spite of countless earlier dummy runs, it stuck four times on the first night and I died four deaths at least. I kept on almost getting on the stage like Miss Worthington. When I finally got on and managed to get out my opening line: 'Are you wondering who I am?' it brought the house down, everyone laughed and I relaxed a good deal. It's curious how misfortune can be such a help.

The play went splendidly and Albert excelled himself. The following morning the press were just as enthusiastic as they'd been in Paris, if not more so, and suddenly it was impossible to get seats for love or money for the whole of the Royal Court season. Actually we were only going to be there for three and a half weeks as we'd now been chosen to go to the Edinburgh Festival, as another show, also scheduled by the English Stage Company, had been abandoned at the last moment.

I dreaded the idea of participating in another Festival, which is, for me, a very unattractive time to visit the Scottish capital. Everything is wildly expensive, and moreover there appears to be no attempt on the part of the natives to jolly things up or infuse an air of gaiety into the proceedings. Apart from the splendid variety of things to see and hear, the tourist is deliberately discouraged from enjoying himself. Hardly a restaurant remains open after eleven and on Sunday the whole city resembles a not absolutely modern morgue. A drink or meal on the Lord's Day is practically unobtainable, unless one has been able to find lodging in one of the better hotels.

We played *Luther* in the Empire Theatre, which I think has now been pulled down and I don't think even Miss Vivien Leigh would have headed a march demanding its preservation as she did about the St James's. It was far away from the centre of the town, over the bridge, and was the largest hall in which we ever played. Deeply confusing after the tiny Royal Court.

It was a huge relief to get back to London town. We had one night off, a Monday, and, by a miracle I was thus not only enabled to do an interview on *Tonight* about *Not on Your Telly!* but also to see *Beyond the Fringe*, which in those days was more difficult to get into than a Scottish Public Hoose on a Sunday.

The following day (5 September 1961) we opened at the Phoenix Theatre, where we enjoyed a good and consistently happy run until 31 March 1962. It was just the right-sized theatre for the piece and I was able to use a door-to-door bus service. Mr Moffatt and I settled down in our cosy dressing-room, divided into two by some curtains, which we could and did draw when we weren't speaking to each other owing to Somebody's disgraceful behaviour during a game of Scrabble. We would generally whip through a game a performance and on matinée days Bill Owen joined us, as he didn't think it quite worthwhile to slip down to his home in Brighton between shows. Perhaps the most enjoyable feature for me about the whole run at the Phoenix was the institution of the bi-weekly matinée tea. This was held in Miss Pamela Brown's lovely apartment in Soho Square, which was just around the corner. Miss B. was away in Rome making a movie, called, so she told us, *Cleopatra*. She was playing the part of the HP (High Priestess) and was away on the HP for about eight months, on and off, which was about the length of our stay in the

Charing Cross Road. She very kindly gave me the keys of the flat and every Wed. and Sat. at 5.45 approx. the Messrs Finney, Cairncross, Moffat and I used to potter across there with any stray people who had or had not seen the matinée, plus friends, relations and lovers. Sometimes to our delight Miss Brown would be there in person, having got one of her occasional leaves of absence from the Eternal Film. When she was present we used to pretend that it wasn't her flat at all and lead her solemnly round, explaining the geography of the house.

As might be imagined with such stout trenchermen the actual food consumed on matinée days was beyond all human belief and each of us vied in providing the richest and most exotic viands. How Mr Finney got through his epileptic fits without throwing up on Weds and Sats will always be a mystery to me. I got in the habit of turning off the loudspeaker during this part of the play, just in case one night the filthy lusts of the flesh might have caught up with him. It was nicest on Saturdays when Mr Moffatt and I (who could stay on) enjoyed both *Juke Box Jury* and *Dixon of Dock Green* before returning to work. Actually we were usually flaked out in a disgusting torpor, which made it difficult to focus properly on the tiny 'idiot box' but the luxury of it was undeniable.

It was a super period in my life and the play did me an undeniable amount of good professionally. I cannot pretend that I found the acting part much easier and I always found the moment before my entrance a severe strain, and the audience could be unaccountable. The part of Tetzel had several dangerous passages, where an interruption was not only possible but permissible. A lady had shouted 'tripe' at Manchester before being ejected and in London there were several Incidents. There was a very spooky matinée when, after I had as usual repeated the line 'Shall I go on?' three times, a voice said 'No' quite firmly, which I must admit threw me considerably. It was a real conversation stopper and it was some time before I brought myself to say, 'Well, I'm going on anyhow,' to which the man replied, 'Why? For God's sake get on with the plot.'

It was a bit disconcerting as up till then I thought I *was* part of the plot but it made the monks laugh, the dear old things.

Throughout the run Albert Finney's sense of self-discipline was deeply impressive and it was astonishing to see how at the ripe age of twenty-five he was able intuitively and without giving offence to keep the standard of the production at a consistently high level. And it is significant that Tony Richardson, unavoidably absent for so much of the run, came to the last performance and pronounced it the best he had ever seen of the play.

10
Tom Jones

I know that people are apt to say that the happiest days of their life were at school or in the war or somewhere equally quaint, but I'm not absolutely sure that my happiest days were not spent in *Tom Jones*, careering up and down the countryside of Britain (South West area), eating myself to a standstill and at times making up my part as I went along. The company was packed with great chums, and John Moffatt and I (still intent on becoming the Basil Radford and Naunton Wayne of the sixties and possibly seventies) were engaged, over high tea as it turned out, to play Thwackum and Square, Master Jones's wildly unattractive tutors. We came more or less straight out of *Luther* and were therefore enabled to embark on our 283rd game of Scrabble on the train to Weymouth, where the film production unit was operating.

It was to prove unlike any film with which I had ever been associated and I gather from everyone else connected with it that they all felt roughly the same way. To begin with, it had been conceived out of love. Both Tony Richardson (director) and John Osborne (script) had adored the Fielding book from childhood and it had been a dream of theirs to bring it to the screen. And when Albert Finney's golden head and talent surfaced so notably, a major problem was automatically solved. The rest of the casting has now passed into legend and at one moment there were five of the ladies appearing in the film being nominated for an Academy Award for the Best Supporting Performance of the Year, which, I believe, is unique in the history of the cinema. They were Dame Edith Evans, Susannah York, Joan Greenwood, Diane Cilento, and Joyce Redman.

The list of stars in it was indeed formidable and many people wonder how it was possible to assemble them, particularly as there was not a single studio shot in the whole film and therefore location stuff was involved. However the British Film Industry was passing through the doldrums in 1962 and Tony Richardson, with charm, tact and cunning, was able to coax a troupe of actors to appear together for him, who dressed the film like a necklace of diamonds. Quite a few of them had never even heard of the book, let alone read it beforehand and, in the early days of the film, a regular vision in the woods at Cranborne (our first location) was a hefty percentage of the cast thumbing their way through the paperback edition of the book to see if Mr Osborne or Mr Sewell Stokes (who contributed some of the additional dialogue) had missed some witticisms or near dittos from the original version.

One of the reasons why so many actors, myself included, are pretty keen on Mr Richardson as a director, is that he occasionally puts his trust in one to the point of lunacy. Who else, pray, would say to Mr Moffatt and myself during a rehearsal: 'Don't think what you are saying now is very funny. Go off, dahlings, and make up something and we'll shoot it.'? So off we'd go and think up a lot of new lines. The trouble was that John, with his infinite experience of W. Shakespeare and Restoration Comedy, would get some authenticity into what he invented, whereas I could do naught but preface everything with 'T'sooth', 'Prithee', or 'By my halibut', which really wouldn't do, as was pointed out by Mr Richardson, to say nothing of Mr Moffatt, always smugly in period.

But there was a day when I sort of got my own back. We were doing a long travelling shot of great intricacy, which involved passing and repassing camera tracks, trees and technicians and making up the dialogue as we went along. Quite suddenly I realized that I wasn't being allowed to get a word in edgeways. Mr Moffatt was indeed going to town in no uncertain fashion. I waited till there was a pausette, grabbed him by the lapels and said:

'Of all the boring things you've ever said since we first met, that last sentence is the most boring.'

'Cut,' said Mr Richardson.

And back we went to our game of Scrabble, where we lost a P in the long grass. Not that we ever did anything else much, except eat ourselves silly, laugh like maniacs and have long zizzes in the afternoon.

But then the whole conception of the film was on a slightly sensual plane. It had started, as far as we were concerned, with a splendid blow-out at the White Elephant for the whole unit and it never let up from that moment on. Indeed I have here in front of me many pink sheets which describe the 'Unit Movement' of *Tom Jones* on Wednesday 27 June 1962. 'The Second assistant, Barry Melrose,' it reads, 'will be in charge of the party and will have a float for the purchase of morning coffee and lunch.' This was the sort of pronouncement that inspired confidence in Mr Moffatt and myself, when we rendezvoused outside the ticket barrier on Platform 10 at Waterloo Station. We had been called for in separate cars as we lived in opposite ends of London. I was called for in the same car as the lovely Miss Susannah York. It said ('Unit Movement' said) I was to be fetched at 0900 and Miss York at 0930. As I can do the distance between our two residences in eight minutes flat on my two flat feet, the time lag seemed excessive but 'Unit Movement' had, I imagine, allowed for the possible delay to be incurred by the unwillingness of Miss Y's dog to accompany us from deepest Chelsea to the wilds of Weymouth. Later it calmed down, after being given an important role in the film. It was called Archie as a matter of fact and tended to get lost a good deal.

But it was all very jolly, this exodus I mean, and even the Southern Railways carriage took on a sort of holiday atmosphere and it was rather like going back from school after the summer term. We had plenty of reading material for the journey with which we had been presented by the production dept, who were headed by the very efficient and delightful Lord Marley, who hates being called that and would rather be addressed as Leigh Amann, and indeed usually is.

There were twenty-nine pages of Roneoed instructions and information to be exact. These ranged from a forbidding section called 'Equipment' to the romantic-sounding 'Dorsetshire and Somerset Locations'. We could see here where everyone was staying.

Tony Richardson was in half Woodsford Castle. Here he was joined of a weekend by his wife, Vanessa Redgrave, and very glamorous parties we used to have on their lawn, or half of it. On the other end of the Housing Plan were J. Curran, P. Ryan and N. Brazier, the 'stunt boys' who were in an eighteen-foot caravan in Nine Yews Stables near Cranborne. It was to be hoped, I imagine, that they weren't all over six foot in length or height or there might have been trouble. Most of the actors and the Unit were lodged in the two main hotels in Weymouth, the Gloucester and the Royal, where the normal residents viewed us with a kind of stunned horror, though the arrival of Dame Edith Evans helped to restore a certain degree of respectability.

The first call sheet of *Tom Jones* read as follows: 'Location EXT: Allworthy's House. Address: Cranborne. Scenes 1–2 (dusk) and 21–25A (inc day).'

Those called for the first day's shooting included the Allworthys (George Devine and Rachel Kempson) and Angela Baddeley, playing Mrs Wilkins, the housekeeper, who finds the infant T. Jones in Squire Allworthy's bed. Albert Finney and David Warner (the odious step-brother Blifil) were called half an hour later with the two actors playing the tutors (the Messrs Moffatt and Bull). Others called were two spaniels, an English setter, a border collie, some Afghan hounds and seven people called A.N. Other who were to stand in for all of us.

Cannot remember what we had to eat the first day but our breath was taken away by the beauty of Cranborne. It has been the property of the Cecil family for well over 300 years, ever since James I presented it to the current owner's ancestors. It is a Manor House and is part of the little town which nestles at its feet. Some of it dates back to King John and the Middle Ages part of the church has stood since 1120. But the house's great charm is that it didn't seem remotely grand in spite of the exquisite walled gardens, rose terraces and carved porches. The rooms and staircases breathed tradition and evoked the past in a remarkable fashion. Yet the general effect was one of reality and intimacy which the film conveyed so truthfully. There was an impressive drive up to the front of the house and a fabulous avenue of yews at the back up which Squire

Western (the ebullient Hugh Griffith) was apt to ride at rather more than a brisk trot.

Yet in spite of the film activity there was a great air of peace about Cranborne and everyone seemed anxious not to disturb it. The entire family was in residence throughout the filming and we were to be there for just over a month. The present Chatelaine, Lady Cranborne, is not only enchanting to behold but a Great Duck. She fell in delightfully with the spirit of it all and seemed genuinely interested in our capers. I hope that she was not too inconvenienced by our advent, as never can property have been lent with such charm and forbearance. Nanny did have to withdraw the children from some of the more explosive members of the unit and it would be nice to visit the house one day without running the risk of tripping over cables and arc lights.

During our stay there props needed (and I quote the call sheets) included 'Flowers to be eaten by horse, a decanter of Madeira Wine, a dead crow and ball for Dog.' On 4 July there was a make-up note. 'Blood and dirt for Tom, Tears for Sophie,' which about sums up the romantic aspect of the plot of *Tom Jones*.

Towards the end of July we pressed on to another beautiful location, though less embedded in tradition and less wooded. The house was called Steepleton and its great advantage, from the camera's point of view, lay in its sweeping lawns and, above all, an enchanting lake for people to fall into, I mean characters in the film of course. The owners were charming and called Robinson. Dame Edith stayed with them and Dame Peggy (Ashcroft) was also a visitor, which gave the whole undertaking a distinguished aura. And even the Elsans, situated at a suitable distance, looked almost sylvan. The grounds, for the purpose of the film, represented Squire Western's property and here was enacted the first love scene between Tom and Sophie, when he gives her the bird, in the strict sense of the phrase. Later, horrid old Blifil (Tom's step-brother), driven by jealousy, lets it out of the cage and Tom falls into the lake, after retrieving it. Blifil laughs at this and Sophie pushes him in too. So a very enjoyable day's filming was had by all, except those actually having to submerge themselves in the slightly murky and be-frogspawned water.

Steepleton was located in the village of Iwerne Steepleton, Blandford Forum and the telephone exchange was called Childe Okeford. We moved on, after a short sojourn, to Cerne Abbas, a picturesque and totally unspoiled village in the heart of Dorset. It was perfect for many film sequences as it had kept its entire High Street intact through the centuries. Apart from the inhabitants having to don period costume, everyone seemed to carry on more or less as usual. At the end of the village there was a large country house, Cerne Abbey in fact, with a marvellous open courtyard at the back. This proved ideal for Squire Western's abode and the Meet. Oh that Meet! What terrifying memories that stirs up. I really loathed my poor steed. In spite of all the lessons, I was still woefully inept as a horseman and fell off many times. To make things dodgier the rain had made the High Street a sort of prolonged bog. I found it extremely difficult to keep my animal on an even keel. I was flanked by the Messrs George Devine and David Warner, gallant but not quite what is known as 'at home' on top of a horse. Who could be, come to think of it? Behind us rode members of the crack Hunt of that part of the world. They were absolutely super but in a tiny bit of a hurry to get cracking. If you bumped into them they were apt to go into a flow of invective and then, suddenly realizing that it was a poor actor and not one of their fellow horsemen, apologize profusely, saying it was *their* fault which was ludicrous. Anyhow it was a dodgy day or two and Johnny Moffatt didn't help matters by having arranged it so that he rode in the Pony and Trap with Miss Allworthy.

The object of this particular sequence was that all should arrive in quick succession to where the Westerns were waiting to greet us, and then proceed up a narrow path to the back of the house to have the Hunt Breakfast. The trouble was that the Allworthy household could only proceed at a snail's pace up the street until finally, in exasperation at so many takes, the horses on which we were riding broke into a brisk gallop and I bit the mud. I bravely remounted, of course.

It was a day of accidents. Even Mr Finney, who maddeningly enough had become an expert rider after about three and a half lessons (it's the same with everything he embarks on: guitar playing, driving, French, and the Twist. Except Scrabble which he plays more slowly than anyone I've ever encountered), well even Mr Finney, as I was saying, was thrown when his horse suddenly reared up in the courtyard. But as there were just the forty-five horses, fifty hounds, geese, donkeys and numerous ordinary dogs all in a very small space, it's amazing nothing really serious went wrong. Tony Richardson had every available camera stationed at various points of vantage and some fairly astonishing shots were obtained. Particularly when Mr Hugh Griffith as the host fell over one of the serving tables and most of the serving ladies, and a general and vastly entertaining mêlée took place on the ground. Mr Griffith's riding double was called Mo Kiki, by the way, though he rode most of the time himself and you may remember a fairly jokey sequence when he came careering up the Allworthy avenue of yews to bite Squire Allworthy's head off. Hugh had slight trouble (after lunch) in mounting his fairly long-suffering steed. It was one of those droll occasions when the bystander catches a glimpse of a head appearing the other side of the horse and then there's a long pause (cameras still turning) until a shove is administered by unseen hands and Hugh was hoisted on as if by jet propulsion. When he finally was well and truly in the saddle he was so cross that he pulled the bridle, and he and his steed went whirling round and round, until the horse got giddy and fell to the ground with Hugh, luckily unhurt. This made a very funny snap and Tony Richardson wisely printed it secretly. It was retained in the ultimate film.

But my falling off wasn't of sufficient interest to be printed and I just went home slightly bruised and determined never to put foot in stirrup again. This was in spite of the presence on the set of Dr Hedley Jones and Mr Michael Woodford (with anaesthetic gun, as it said on the call sheet). But I suspect that the latter was a vet. Two dear old St John's Ambulance men were in attendance as well, but practically always near the Catering Vans. Look who's talking!

Shortly after these stirring events we moved to Melbury Park for the filming of the actual Stag Hunt. This was part of the vast property of Lord and Lady Ilchester, who also own a considerable portion of Kensington. They were extremely hospitable and showed us every courtesy. I don't think they had come across a lot of actors before and their attitude to them was occasionally a little curious.

'You are bores going on Friday,' said Milady one day to some of us. 'I've got some people coming down for the weekend and it would have been so nice to have sent them out to play with you, while I got on with the weeding.'

Tony Richardson had hired a helicopter for the sequence and sent the Ilchesters up in it to fly over their impressive demesne. We waited breathlessly for her comment.

'It was very interesting,' she told Mr R., 'because it enabled one to see which of the trees were dead and needed to be taken away.'

We were all pretty alarmed by the helicopter because one of the call sheets said: 'Only those people directly requested to approach this machine should do so. All other personnel please stay clear of the helicopter blades.'

It was as if it had been a real person and might have said, 'Look here, Bull, approach me.' All a bit spooky as it looked like some vast prehistoric bird among the trees. Albert liked it very much though, and on one of the few occasions when he wasn't required for a spell, he took the opportunity to whizz skywards. The film camera was still in the machine, with a few feet of film left, so Mr Finney proceeded to take some vibrant shots of the penis belonging to the Giant of Cerne Abbas, a curiously formed and pagan relic engraved on the side of a hill.

Lady Cranborne joined us for the Stag Hunt and was as delightful as ever. She had decided she still hadn't had too much of us and very spectacular she looked riding side-saddle and, as she is an expert horsewoman, she much embellished the picture. But she was the unconscious cause of a good deal of labour trouble.

One day she came over to our caravan and said, 'Look here, Tony Richardson has asked me to jump a five foot nine inch fence. It's higher than anything in the Grand National. I don't mind having a bash but do you think I ought to do it for two guineas a day?' It was said mainly jokingly. But we were horrified at hearing of the daily wage she and the rest of the Wiltshire and Dorsetshire aristocracy were getting. We told her that she could get at least twenty-five pounds Danger Money for a start.

That set the whole thing off. Egged on by the stunt men, our distinguished Hunting Set went on a sort of strike. It was finally settled, but the scenes were completed in a slightly more frigid atmosphere than had existed at the beginning. The trouble with the film throughout was the astonishing mixture between the amateur and the professional. And in this case there was no doubting the efficiency of the riders. And the days were long, exhausting and repetitive. I don't propose to go into the details of What Happened to the Stag and certain aspects of this part of the shooting of the film because I have nightmares still of Incidents. And I'm not even mad about animals.

During the hunting scenes we all had to sit on a saddle on the back of a little van and pretend we were on a real horse. The van was pulled backwards by another vehicle on which the camera was fairly perilously perched. At the sides of the van we were in, members of the county rode at full gallop to give the scenes verisimilitude. It was a form of riding I liked v. much indeed and, as I thrashed about with my whip and yelled a great many oaths and exhortations, I felt no end of a dog. It went on for what seemed like ages and made for extremely monotonous viewing in the ball room at the Gloucester Hotel, Weymouth where the 'rushes' were shown.

One of my favourite simple jokes is about somebody bringing the infant Moses to Pharoah who said he thought it was the most ghastly-looking child. 'Oh, but,' the man said, 'it looked frightfully good in the rushes.' Anyhow, the nights with these close-up shots of us on the back of the van went on endlessly. In fact they went on so long that a percentage of the audience zizzed off. After about an hour of actors', horses', dogs' and stags' faces in continuous close-up there was quite suddenly a shot of Tom Courtnay striding across those Borstal Woods in *The Loneliness of the Long Distance Runner*.

This bit was in black and white and had been thrown in by the editor as a joke. Dame Edith Evans, next to whom I was sitting, awoke with a start. She viewed Mr Courtnay with a slightly disapproving glare.

'Good gracious!' said the great actress, sitting bolt upright. 'What part does *he* play?'

The next night the amount of film to be shown was so long that we had to have an Intermission. The lights went up and, as in a real cinema, young ladies sauntered up and down the aisle crying, 'Choc-ices, Cigarettes, Coffee'. Though in this case they were the waitresses from the hotel.

But not all the shots were shown and one or two, though exquisitely funny in themselves, were literally unprintable. Such a one was the remarkable afternoon when our dear director got his come-uppance for encouraging the artistes to improvise.

The scene in which this occurred was the one where the naughty Molly (lush, beautiful Diane Cilento), goes to church accompanied by her very apparent pregnancy. Her arrival naturally scandalizes the entire congregation and when they come out of church there is a Demonstration. Waiting outside are a bevy of the villagers. Now most of these were played in the film by real residents (in this case from Nettlecombe village, Somerset) including indeed the vicar's wife and the squire. But in order to ensure reality and distinction, there were a selection of professional actresses heading them, led by that droll and marvellous lady, Barbara Hicks.

So there was Mr Richardson before the take explaining to Miss Hicks in his usual seemingly haphazard but uniquely successful way what he wanted from her.

'Now, Barbara, dahling, I leave it all to you. You've got to lead all these people. You've got to show all the hatred and jealousy you feel for this dreadful girl. You see, she's let down the whole village and you're all *furious*. But also you rather envy her because she's been had by Tom Jones and you haven't.'

'I see,' said Miss Hicks. 'But what do I say?'

'It doesn't matter, dahling. Whatever you say will be just right, I know it.'

Mr Richardson left her to go back to the camera and a few minutes later gave the command 'Action'. We all filed out of the church and Molly came last on the arm of Black George, her father (played by that miraculous actor, Wilfred Lawson).

Miss Hicks emerged from behind a tombstone, took up an extremely large clod of earth, threw it at Molly and yelled at the top of her voice:

'Take that, you eighteenth-century c—t!'

And that's why, dear children, the sound in the film seems to go a bit funny round about that moment. It finished all of us off, I don't mind telling you, and Miss Hicks just stood there with a seraphic smile on her face saying, 'I always dreamed of the day when I'd be allowed to do something like that and now it's happened.'

Earlier in the day we had been filmed inside the church and I was sitting just in front of the vicar's wife (for real). I heard part of the conversation in progress and suddenly she announced a little wistfully that she'd never seen the church so full since her husband had taken the living over.

'Yes,' said a slightly nervous but cultured voice from beside her, 'and never so many denominations I suppose. Catholics, Methodists, Christian Scientists and Prostitutes. I mean Protestants,' it added hurriedly.

Earlier in the day we had had rather a macabre experience. While we were rehearsing burying Miss Bridget Allworthy in the actual graveyard, we were asked to desist for half an hour, while a real burial took place.

We had by now moved yet again and you'll be surprised to learn that our new home was to be at St Audrey's Junior School, Nettlecombe Court, near Williton, Somerset. It had its own church and for many years had been the family home of the Trevelyan family. There were still relics of great grandeur and some of the rooms were magnificently panelled. Many of the staircases and fireplaces had remained undisturbed, and with the brilliance of the art dept (headed by Ralph Brinton and Ted Marshall) the atmosphere was authentic and exciting. We dressed in dormitories and there was even a matron's room which naturally Dame Edith Evans was allowed to annex as her dressing-room. Nettlecombe was used for a variety of settings, from Newgate Jail to the exterior of the inn at Upton. Most of the bedrooms in the film (and you may remember one or forty of those) were shot here and the fantastic eating scene took place here and was, for the record, largely the invention of Miss Redman and Mr Finney, the protagonists.

The unit's headquarters were now mainly in Taunton, as it was handier, and we were not sorry to leave Weymouth. It was easier to get to London and accommodation was so scarce in the area that the production dept were quite pleased to release us as soon as they could. In Weymouth they were keen on us staying until they were absolutely certain we couldn't be used in the next few days. Even if one was told one could go, it was not outside the realms of possibility to be pulled off the train just as it was starting. In fact Mr Moffatt and I used to go down as far as we could and get in the first carriage of all. You may think that one was bored by now which isn't the case. It was just that it was nice to get a breather and rush back to London to have a look at one's window-boxes or something.

Taunton was much less personal and I was lucky to spend most of my nights in a very remote hotel at a place called Holford Coombe. One hit one's head a good deal on the ceiling but otherwise it was enchanting and quiet. By now one felt a very old campaigner indeed and we had amassed a great many camp followers from the various locations we'd visited. I sometimes wonder what damage we did unwittingly. What with the stunt gentlemen's irresistible appeal to the local ladies and the fact that filming seemed 'such fun' we must have unhinged and changed many a simple country outlook. I only hope that the streets of London aren't being walked on by milkmaids, who have come to the capital for fame and fortune, in expectation of emulating Miss F. Hill. I do know that one lad, of previously ruddy cheeks and healthy mien, was last glimpsed by me as a croupier in one of the seedier gambling joints in the Earls Court area.

After the film was completed, rumours went whizzing around about the product. The air was so rife with reports that it was uncuttable, dull, a mess, had no chance of general distribution, etc., etc., that United Artists who had largely backed it were alarmed. Mr Richardson went quietly about cutting it with Tony Gibbs, and engaged Michael MacLiammoir as commentator, speeded up some of the film to a Keystone Cop pace, took out masses of extraneous dialogue, and the rest is cinema history. Bunged into the London Pavilion, the usual home of horror films, it ran just the year and, at the height of its triumph, the queues encircled the block. In New York its success was so immense that it was shown at two cinemas next door to each other. But there again no one had foreseen its triumph. In my opinion, and it's impertinent of me to make a pronunciamento, it is a film of the utmost courage and ingenuity and probably nothing really like it will ever be seen again. Not that it won't be imitated (I hear with foreboding that someone is going to have a bash at *Moll Flanders*. To say nothing of *Fanny Hill!*) but I doubt that anyone will ever be able to arrange the sequence of fortuitous blendings of talent which went to the making of *Tom Jones*.

Speaking for myself, I had what can only be described as a ball.

11
Pickwick

Towards the end of the London run of *Luther* I was approached vaguely about appearing in a proposed musical version of *The Pickwick Papers*. It was to be directed by Peter Coe, who had had something of a triumph dealing with the same author's *O. Twist*. Now the one wish that practically every straight actor has is to be in a musical entertainment and pretty disastrous it can be if this wish is granted.

All right! All right! I can practically hear you hissing, 'What about Rex Harrison then?' That's different, dears. I happen to know that Mr H. studied singing for at least a year before *My Fair Lady* and that relaxed and apparently effortless performance was due to intense hard work combined with supreme technique.

With me the problem is slightly enlarged by my being tone deaf for a start, so I told Mr Coe's assistant that I really couldn't sing a note, but he persuaded me to come along anyhow. I boarded a 22 omnibus with a piece of music and the *New Musical Express* under my arm to show willing and what I meant to do was this: Stride straight on to the stage of the Saville Theatre as bold as brass and say to Mr Coe and any other bystanders, I am now going to sing 'Love Will Find a Way' from *The Maid of the Mountains*. No accompaniment, thank you,' I would add, with a charming smile at the pianist, and then I'd let 'em have it:

Whate'er befall I still recall that sunlit mountain side,
Where skies are blew and hearts are trew and love's the only guide.
If faithful to my friends I stay, no thought can fill me with dismay,

Love holds the key to set me free
And love will find a way.

After this I would steal quietly out of the building and take a 22 bus home. This, I imagined, would ensure that I probably wouldn't be asked to appear in a musical for some time, which would spare me heartbreak. The role I was under consideration for in *Pickwick* had just the five numbers to sing.

But all my self-destructive plans were to come to nothing. I wasn't even allowed to get on to the stage or indeed get 'Love Will Find a Way' from under my armpit. Mr Coe caught me by the arm as I was trying to sneak past.

'I've had a better idea,' he said. 'What about Sergeant Buzfuz?'

He handed the script to me, told me to read it and let him know what I thought about it. Truth to tell I hadn't looked at the book since I had played old Tony Weller in a TV series. The court scene wasn't in that version as far as I can remember so all I knew about the part was that both Bransby Williams and Sir Donald Wolfit had done it up hill and down dale in various media, sometimes as solo turns. So I read the musical version with a certain amount of curiosity. The part of Buzfuz I found was vastly similar to Tetzel in many ways. To begin with, it was a long tirade of around eight minutes and superbly written. It was only in one scene, the Bardell versus Pickwick court scene, which, placed almost at the end of the show, was the climax of the entertainment.

I must say I was very attracted by the whole idea. Here was a non-singing part in a musical starring Harry Secombe and one could not foresee the remotest possibility of it failing. But I was playing for higher stakes as I wanted desperately to go to New York in *Luther*. I had as yet signed no contract for this though it appeared fairly certain that I would be asked to go. *Pickwick* was scheduled to open in Manchester at the beginning of June 1963 and come into London a month later. As *Luther* was due to open in America during the first few weeks of September you can realize that the time-margin was very small indeed.

So that was my position, and fairly dodgy it was, you must admit.

But in show-business, when one is in a dilemma, Fate with a capital F tends to take a Firm hand and relieves you of the hideous responsibility of Making a Choice.

Philip Pearman, my mentor, took the reins with Father Figure Fate and to my astonishment (and certainly his) landed the most sensational contract I've ever had. I was given a get-out clause by which I could leave the play *after only four weeks in London* (the italics are not mine, but the printers' if they can find them). It was a staggering concession because it meant that not only could I go to America, should a firm offer come, but I was not bound indefinitely to *Pickwick*.

Yet the boost to my professional life was nothing to the delight of getting to know Harry Secombe. I know I have been constantly accused of having a 'star' complex, and indeed I have, there are no two ways about that. I suppose it goes back to my school days when I used to write to Mrs Siddons. I stand in awe of the gorgeous creatures until I meet them 'in person' and then there are no half-lengths. I either dote on them with an embarrassing and cow-like (that can't be correct usage) devotion, or tend to dismiss them as being stupid, conceited, selfish, or 'rather sad', and sometimes all three and a half. If I take the latter course of analysis it is because I have been either ignored, snubbed or, in rare cases, bored. But in fact I am hardly ever disappointed.

Now H. Secombe Esq., CBE is something quite exceptional in the star line. To begin with, you never hear anything but the most extravagant things said about him. 'Oh, Harry Secombe, he's lovely,' a tough character will say, and I've never caught anyone saying a bitchy, unkind or ungenerous word about him. And this is absolutely unknown in our business.

So having digested all this, I was fascinated to see what this supposed paragon was really like. Somehow he sounded too good to be true and, filthy sceptic that I am, I thought he might turn out to be one of those 'professional good sorts', who are so deeply disturbing. These types, with their jokes and smiling masks, are lurking Beasts capable of stopping *your* laughs, if any, stealing your wife, lover, or last stick (of greasepaint).

But Harry is a Great Man and I use the capitals advisedly because so far in my lifetime I have met no one to compare with him for utter unselfishness and generosity, combined with an innate and unboring goodness. No one would think of doing the things which he does at times when one would imagine he would have no occasion for selflessness. The coffee and sandwiches at three in the morning, produced out of the air, after a particularly gruelling dress rehearsal when all, including Harry, are on their knees, for example.

It is Harry who will, by doing something excruciatingly funny at exactly the right moment, avert a temperament, row or scene. Not that there were many during the rehearsals of *Pickwick*, thanks to Harry and Peter Coe, who wisely ruled with a rod of iron. In musical productions there are so many people with fingers in the pie that tempers and vast areas of time are expended needlessly.

I was hardly required to rehearse at all. I went off to the costumiers and got my court gown (or rather Mr Robert Morley's from the film *Libel*) and about once a week bashed through the speech in a semi-defiant way. It was all a bit frightening as a matter of fact but there was not much point in rehearsing it without the set. And as the designer was Mr Sean Kenny the set was a great many ingenious trucks whizzing on and off like dodgem cars. The actors had to push them about and highly dangerous they looked. Fortunately we had a full week with the full sets at Manchester before we opened. We were to be six weeks there (four actually playing) and I took a flat out at Stretford as I had some writing to do (ha! ha!) and went on a diet (ha! ha! again). I did for myself, if that's the phrase, and there was a garden, and the time passed very pleasantly. I flew up to London nearly every weekend usually on the same plane as Mr Secombe, who begrudged every minute away from his enchanting wife and family.

He is one of the few deeply religious actors I know and, though he never rams his faith down one's throat, his influence is always there and I felt very ashamed of myself when I once underestimated it. A notice went up on the board one day at the Palace Theatre about a short service being held on the stage before the performance. Harry is the pillar of the Actors' Church Union and I remember thinking, 'Oh dear, no one will turn up out of this lot and Harry'll be disappointed.' So, with great pomposity and smugness, I slipped into the theatre to lend my presence, only to find a big turnout. Grumpy character actors, frivolous young ladies of the ensemble, the odd musician and stage hand, came out from behind bits of scenery (or in this case bits of trucks) and it was a moving ten minutes. Harry read the Lesson and then we gave thanks for everything, including the success of *Pickwick*.

And for that I felt we should have thanked Harry. The triumph of the play was entirely due to him. What few people realize is that *The Pickwick Papers* has always proved tricky as stage material. Till the musical version it has never had any sort of success. Charles Laughton played Mr P. in one version in London, and George Howe in another in New York. James Hayter had a go in an Ealing film, and Sir Henry Irving used portions of Jingle for a curtain-raiser.

Till Harry played it, I have always thought its failure was due to the fact that the principal character is purely a literary one. When brought to life, it would seem that Mr Pickwick is made rings round dramatically by the subsidiary personalities like Jingle, Sam Weller, Snodgrass, Mrs Bardell and even the Fat Boy. But in the musical, with the songs and Mr Secombe's tremendous voice, the part took on a new dimension, and such a wave of warmth, friendliness and enjoyment came wafting over the footlights that it was practically impossible for the audience not to be swept away. He has that knack of conveying happiness and well-being that really does set your senses singing and your heart dancing.

It was a fairly smooth and uneventful opening in Manchester. We had a charity preview on Whit Sunday, 1963, when the microphones were so ill adjusted that even the mayor couldn't hear a word. I can't think why I say 'even the mayor' because he really must be deafened by all those toastmasters and towncriers. But by Monday all was well, except that there was the usual heat wavette, which always seems to attend costume-play openings. The press next day were fairly enthusiastic but regretted that Harry Secombe gave such a restrained performance! Teddy Green (Sam Weller) scored an enormous success on the first night and was brilliant, full of sexy cheekiness and dancing superbly. He got wonderful notices and Harry was genuinely delighted.

Gradually during the month we played the Palace, he stopped being overawed by the occasion and splendid bits of Secombe began to creep in, all of which Mr Pickwick might easily have thought of himself. All right! All right! How do *you* know that the original character didn't turn a mean cartwheel in the privacy of his bedroom? The audience adored him and, by the time we were due to open in London, it was fairly obvious that the show couldn't fail to be a big hit. There were many brilliant supporting performances, as Mr P. Coe had deliberately chosen actors who could sing and not vice versa. Apart from the electric Mr Green, there were Anton Rogers's Jingle, Julian Orchard's Snodgrass, Jessie Evans's Mrs Bardell and Robin Wentworth's Tony Weller, none of which could have been bettered in my opinion. There were many others who contributed much to the entertainment. And me? How nice of you to ask! I repeated my *Luther* performance, only louder because it was a musical. I think at best I was adequate but it was a bit lazy and haphazard. I even got dear Jess Evans to put the black on my eyes, which was my only contribution in the way of make-up.

I enjoyed it all hugely and after a bit didn't get as panic-struck as I usually do. Subconsciously I suppose I knew that Harry would be more than adequate to deal with any emergency that might arise. Not that I dared to look at him much when I was delivering my tirade. He had a knack of doing things that would have paralysed me into hopeless and embarrassing laughter if I'd once relaxed, and there is a way in which he twists his mouth like Plasticine into a camp sneer, which finishes me off.

My nearest approach to hysteria used to come regularly every performance at the end of the court scene, when there was a number called 'British Justice' which we all sang. I say 'all' but in fact it was sung by the entire company *except* me. I started to sing it very early on during rehearsals but then was asked, quite charmingly, by several proper singers if I would desist as it put them off, my changing key and all that sort of jazz. The number was sung with the

Prosecution on one side of the stage and the defence on the other. In order to make it not too obvious that I was not singing and thus place me in a humiliating position, I used to open my Prosecution mouth, look right back to the stalls of the Saville Theatre (to avoid catching Harry's eye as a matter of fact) and mime the words. I thought I was pretty good at this, until one day Marcus Dodds, our delightful Mus. Dir., drew me aside after a performance and said to me:

'Look here, Peter, I forgot to tell you. We've altered it a bit and now each side of the stage sings alternate lines of "British Justice" so will you kindly keep your trap shut when your side of the stage is *not* singing.'

When the time came to make a long-playing gramophone record of the show I was not wildly surprised at not being asked to the recording session, but I was deeply touched at being awarded a minute percentage of the takings. It was pointed out disarmingly that I had contributed to the success of the show and every now and again, as a result, I get a tidy tiny sum for *not* singing on a gramophone record, which seems the height of chic to me. The record has been a great success incidentally and for weeks you couldn't turn on the radio without hearing Harry telling us what he'd do if he Ruled the World. I only wish he would. Rule the world, I mean.

It was far and away the most comfortable engagement I've ever enjoyed. I could leave my flat after the curtain had gone up and still be sure of getting to the theatre in plenty of time. Matinées were at three o'clock so one had plenty of time for a good tuck-in before the show and a good zizz after.

So you can imagine how loath I was to leave *Pickwick*. It was a marvellous company and I blubbed a bit at a partyette I gave on the last night. Harry gave me my first pair of gold cuff-links when I left. But I fancy, at the time of writing, that it's not the last I've heard of that particular musical. And I am praying it's not the last I've heard of Mr Secombe, bless his cotton socks!

A few weeks after saying goodbye, when I was lying on my bed in a hotel room in Philadelphia and feeling extremely low, the phone went and I heard a lovely gurgle from the other side of the Atlantic. It was Harry ringing up after a matinée of *Pickwick* to ask me if I was all right. He seemed to have, as usual, a large percentage of cast in his dressing-room, and I felt warmed, grateful and very very homesick.

PART FOUR

Bull Fever

12
Perilous Journey

Once a year my mother, now a rising eighty-seven, pops off to a nice country-house hotel near Heathfield in Sussex. She dreads her 'holiday' and it is really only at the pistol-point of domestic necessity that she can bring herself to leave her comfortable Chelsea flat. Yet once she has arrived in her place of exile she settles down fairly happily, as her hosts are kind and genuinely fond of her. In fact everything goes swimmingly during the entire three weeks, as long as no one requires a bath at the same time as my mother. Her interest in new residents is not confined to their appearance or even love life but mainly to what time they LOOK like wanting a bath.

Preparations for her departure are elaborate and intensive and start many weeks before. Everything is carefully planned and it is no fault of hers that what should be quite a simple operation is marred every time by unforeseen perils.

Her exodus on this occasion was a typical example. For the last few years she has caught, with about an hour to spare, the 10.38 to Heathfield from Victoria, but never without some hair-raising hazard. Last year she was put by a nonchalant porter in the wrong half of the train and had to change at Eridge, wherever that may be. The year before she was deliberately dispatched, protesting, on the 10.08. It got to Heathfield very much earlier but it threw my mother who had contracted with herself to catch the 10.38.

I usually pick her up in a taxi at 09.45 hours ('that should give us plenty of time, dear' and indeed it does). This enables us to arrive at Victoria Station well before 10.00 hours, when there is scant chance of the train condescending to show its dear little face on the platform.

The trek on this occasion had started off well enough with the trapping of an amiable but bemused taxi-gentleman, who had just finished transporting an eccentric lady client. She had apparently asked him what she owed. He had replied 'Three shillings and six-pence, Madam' civilly enough but the lady had flown into a rage and shouted: 'You are insulting. How do you know that I am married?' The driver had wisely held his peace but was obviously relieved to pick up a fairly normal consignment like the mater and me.

We arrived at the Buckingham Palace entrance to the station in the highest spirits at 09.52 hours and if I hadn't had my mother's horoscope for the day engraven on my brain, I would have imagined that all boded well. It had read: 'A puzzling day. Special compensations await you after tea!'

There were two porters ready to take the luggage whom I shall have to christen Porter A and Porter B. They have leading parts in the ensuing drama and do not deserve to linger in the memory anonymously.

'What train, Madam?' asked Porter A cordially.

'The 10.38 to Heathfield,' replied my mother.

Porter A looked at Porter B with consternation written all over his face.

'There is no such train, Madam,' he said.

'Nonsense,' replied my mother. 'I booked my seat on it at the Army and Navy Stores yesterday.'

Both porters were visibly rattled by this piece of intelligence but Porter B rallied:

'There is a 10.08 and an 11.08 to Heathfield,' he said helpfully but ungrammatically.

'But the Army and Navy,' reiterated my mother, 'told me that the 10.38 was definitely running.'

'You should have checked with OUR enquiries, Madam,' chimed in Porter A, re-entering the fray.

A short silence followed, only to be broken by the kindlier porter (B).

'Why not take the 10.08?' he pleaded.

My mother, still on her guard but pretty off her porter (A) asked coldly if it went straight through to Heathfield.

'No, Madam,' came the reply. 'You would have to change at Eridge!'

'In that case,' said my mother with ill-concealed triumph in her voice, 'I would rather take the 11.08. The Army and Navy told me that DID go through!'

The porters, to my surprise, did not question this statement and I seized the lull in hostilities to suggest that the luggage should be parked in the cloakroom and that we should have a strong cup of coffee. I did not however include Porters A to B in the invitation.

Porter A disappeared with the luggage after a dainty shrug and left us with mixed emotions. Suddenly my mother and I were galvanized by a quiet voice behind us saying:

'Which platform for the 10.38 to Heathfield, please Porter?'

I whipped round to see Porter B staring thunderstruck at a lady in sensible tweeds. It was some time before he could pull himself together and then he bawled at his friend Porter A, now deep in conversation with Cloakroom:

'Hold it, Bill. Here's another for that 10.38.'

The tone of his voice suggested that Sensible Tweeds and my mother had asked to be transported on a rocket train to the Moon and were querying which end the rocket restaurant car would be situated in. Nevertheless Porter A returned to us and dumped my mother's luggage gloomily round and about my feet. He then instructed Porter B to Go and Inquire. In his absence my mother struck up an immediate and warm friendship with Sensible Tweeds and questions like, 'What are things coming to?' and 'What will the foreigners think?' came wafting across the station air with crystal clarity.

After what seemed an age we spotted Porter B winging his way wearily over to us, holding a scruffy piece of paper.

'Platform 14,' he announced simply and unaffectedly.

My mother made no comment on this *volte face*, to my amazement, beyond pointing out that last year it had been platform 16. A small excited cavalcade (we had now been joined by a lady

with a small trim beard, both of whom were bound for Uckfield)
moved off to platform 14, where, needless to say, there was no sign of
a train and the barriers were closed.

The porters dropped the luggage, intending presumably to have a
short conference on the mutability of human affairs. Unfortunately
they found themselves caught up in the web of uncertainty which
seemed to be sweeping Victoria Station like a forest fire. Passengers
from nowhere descended on them for information, little knowing
that they could not have picked two more unreliable authorities.

At long last a gentleman appeared from a trap-door inside the
platform and opened the barriers. As we surged forwards he
hurriedly closed them. But to compensate for the disappointment he
did insert a destination board into the socket provided. It read 'Front
Part Uckfield. Rear Part Heathfield'!

I turned to my mother with relief.

'Well, dear, that looks all right,' I said.

'Last year,' she replied coldly, 'it was the other way round and I got
into the wrong part and had to change at Eridge!'

Before I had had time to work this out, the barriers opened and we
were allowed on to the platform just in time to receive the onslaught
of several hundred tardy daily-breaders who were disgorged by an
angry-looking train. They knocked a suitcase and a porter sideways
but luckily not the mater, who stood her ground. She surveyed the
train with disfavour.

'What a dirty train,' she commented.

'It's probably not the right one,' I said facetiously and a second
later could have bitten off my tiny tongue. For looking back at the
barrier I saw a Hand stretch out and withdraw the destination board
on which all our hopes were centred.

'I don't want to seem too inquisitive,' I said to Porter B, 'but why
have they taken that board down?' I had established a sort of
relationship with both porters by now owing to the fact that
they had seen me recently in an unsuitable film called *Salute the
Toff*.

Porter B loped off to the barrier and consulted an unknown
Spokesman for British Railways. He returned with his cheeks

suffused by a blush which certainly became the sensational announcement he was about to make.

'Platform 15,' he said in a fine clear voice.

My mother, to my astonishment, started giggling and I loved her very dearly at that moment. Her only comment, before sounding the retreat, was to repeat her assertion that last year it had been platform 16.

13
Egos and Alter Dittos

It's curious how devastating an effect can be caused by an innocent remark, if it is badly timed. How often have *you* been furious when someone has said: 'How well you're looking,' when you are in fact feeling ghastly or recovering from a hangover. The reverse is also true. 'You look a bit pale. Are you sure you're all right?' when for once you're on top of the world and in the very pink of condition.

Then there is the direct attack. 'You *have* put on weight,' or 'How *thin* you've got,' are pronounciamenta which come to other people's lips far too readily, not that the second phrase has ever been, or is indeed likely to be, addressed to me alas!

Another conversational hazard is the identity gambit.

'You're exactly like somebody I used to know in the Army' is a line which tends to make me dislike the speaker at sight, or rather sound. He usually delivers it with a slightly condescending smile and intonation as if he were conferring a great honour on one. He rarely elaborates on the likeness or submits an identi-kit of his friend's character, but I don't think there is anyone in the world who wants to be told that he (or she) has a double lurking around. There is something spooky in the idea, and the phrase 'spitting image' has never endeared itself to me. Another hopeless and unanswerable opener is: 'It *is* you, isn't it?' usually spoken by a face one has never seen in one's life and hopes never to see again.

Being an actor one is frequently accosted by total strangers who are convinced that they know you personally, having met you on midget screens in lounges, bedrooms or mother-in-laws' houses.

Usually the encounter starts with a penetrating stare which induces one to think that one may not have adjusted one's dress properly, as is *de rigueur* in some of the better class conveniences. After this the braver specimens advance for a verbal attack.

'I know you, don't I?' is a familiar approach. I tend to remain impassive and totally unhelpful, favouring them nonetheless with a quizzical but wry smile.

After several floundering sentences they usually give up and say, 'I know the face but . . .' and their voices trail off, leaving them temporarily at a loss. If they look nice or, I'm afraid, beautiful, I come to their rescue and volunteer my name, but frequently this step is a disaster for both parties. They look even more puzzled and are, I think, convinced that I've given them an alias, and I might tell you that the whole incident isn't inclined to give my morale much of a boost. So I just look sadly at them and slink away, hoping that they may imagine that I'm one of those lovely wrestlers who bite each other on Saturday afternoons, while I am waiting to check my football pools. Funnily enough I did tell one enquirer that I was Tom Jones and he didn't seem in the least surprised. So anything is possible.

Sometimes the assailant is certain that he (or she) knows more about you and your career than you do yourself and it's a tidge depressing to be assured over and over again that one has been seen in both *Oliver* and *A Man for All Seasons*, when one hasn't in fact even been approached about playing a role in either of these splendid entertainments on stage or screen.

'Oh, but you *were* in it,' the idiots insist, even after I've assured them that they are mistaking me for some other ample character artiste. Quite often it's less exhausting to say, 'All right then. I *was* in it,' which sends *them* happily away anyhow. Or even pretend I'm someone else. I've been Robert Morley, Willoughby Goddard, John Sutro and even Orson Welles more times than I can count.

But in our profession we really are up against it when it comes to the layman (or laywoman if there is such a word) and their idea of what the actor *does*. 'Do you have to do it every night?' (If it happens to be a West End play.) 'Does the make-up hurt?' and 'How do you

know when it's your turn to speak?' are typical examples of the
questions one is asked at parties and things. Which reminds me of
what Dan Massey said to the silly young girl who asked him at a
party, 'Don't you get tired of saying the same thing every night?'
Replied Mr Massey, 'Yes, don't you?'

And heaven help you if you are in a television programme which
has displeased the majority of the viewers. In the days when there
were still greengrocers, butchers, florists and fishmongers in my part
of the King's Road, Chelsea, I had to be very careful what engage-
ments I accepted, or I'd be greeted by a subsequent storm of abuse.

'The things you do for money nowadays.' 'F—ing awful show you
were in last night,' and 'Hello Strangler' were comments handed out
gratuitously. And sometimes on these occasions one was forced
back indoors to face possible starvation. But appear in a popular
series and the world was your oyster and at the fishmonger's the
reverse was possible.

As a matter of fact there has recently been an upward trend in my
relationship with *my* public. Owing to a series of fortuitous
circumstances, I was engaged to participate in a commercial for the
box to advertise a product called 'Fish Fingers'. The short film was an
immediate success and to my huge financial (and of course artistic)
delight was shown many times a day. The result was that, although
no one had the faintest idea of my real name, I was immediately
identifiable and my stage name was written on many hearts. Daily I
was pursued down the street by urchins yelling, 'There goes good old
Commodore Bird's Eye.'

I only hope my most unfavourite non-fan saw it. I ran into him the
other month when I was coming out of the laundry, minding my
own washing and doing nobody any harm.

' 'Ello,' said a voice just behind me. I turned to face a cheerful man
waiting near the bus stop.

'You 'aven't been very busy lately, 'ave you?' the voice continued.

Now this is the sort of thing which makes me absolutely livid.
There is a certain type of viewer who cannot believe there *is* any
other medium of entertainment besides the Idiot Box. I explained to
the man that an actor did have media outside the small screen in

which he could find employment if he was lucky. I hurriedly assured him that I was one of these and during the last year had indeed been exceptionally busy. I'd been starring opposite the Burtons in Hollywood, and had but recently returned from playing the lead in a big Broadway musical. I had a best-selling novel just published in the States and was about to condense the life of George Best into a twenty-four-part serial.

I stopped this tissue of lies, shaking with rage and clutching my laundry with abandon. There was a pause while he studied me pityingly.

'Yeah,' he said, 'but you 'aven't been on telly, 'ave you?' I felt I should have been in the dock with the Brothers Kray, so guilty did he make me feel. If I'd known what bus he'd been catching I would have pushed him under it and probably ended up in the dock myself. I could see that he was not the man to be impressed by the fact that I was the voice of 'Kattomeat'. I'm frightfully impressed myself.

This disagreeable incident would probably not have happened a few months later when I'd established myself as Commodore Bird's Eye, though I expect he would have mixed me up with Keith Michell in the *Wives of Henry VIII* ... After all they were both costume jobs. Mark you I like the idea of being easily identifiable as Commodore Bird's Eye and I only hope the Fish Fingers people do too and will whirl me off again one day to the Barbados to shoot Episode Two. After all I'm well known for my interpretations of service gentlemen. For a long time I was Colonel Ironmonger. Oh, didn't you know? Well, it all started like this:

There was, and indeed still is, an excellent entertainment guide called *What's On in London*. It has been in existence for many years and has a gossip column giving news of future productions both on stage and screen. It also mentions actors and actresses fairly frequently and at one point certain names seemed to appear regularly and I got a tiny bit exasperated by this, possibly because mine never featured. An actor who seemed to get more than his share of publicity was Martin Benson. He always appeared to have not only one job in the offing but several. Phrases which started off,

'Martin Benson cannot make up his mind whether to ... or ...' were not likely to cause the out of work actor to rub his hands in glee. So I decided to have a bit of fun, though I have nothing against Mr Benson himself, who has written books on acting so he must know what it's all about. I thought I couldn't very easily write to *What's On* under my own name or they'd smell a rat, so one fine day I decided to become Colonel Ironmonger.

It was the Colonel who wrote to the magazine to say that he had but recently returned to England after a long period of service in the Far East and could *What's On* possibly help him? He and his wife were avid theatregoers and would very much like to find out where a particular favourite of theirs, Martin Benson, was appearing. They had, of course, followed his film career with interest in various camp cinemas and had speculated as to whether he was or was not related to the late Sir Frank Benson, the distinguished cricketer-actor-manager. Had *What's On* an answer to his enquiries?

Yes, it had, and a letter came whizzing back saying exactly what Mr Benson was doing at that very moment and in the months to come. This early success went to both the Colonel's and my head and after that there was no holding us. I felt a wonderful sense of power in having an *alter ego* entirely at my disposal. I suppose that Baron Frankenstein must have undergone a similar emotion when he created another being out of nothing.

But haven't some of *you* wanted to record on paper your indignation at a person or persons, and been stopped from doing so by a desire to remain anonymous? There you are, with your poison-pen poised in mid-air and suddenly you realize that you'd rather not put *your* name at the bottom of the page. And yet it seems rather abortive and weak to sign it 'Disgusted', 'Mother of Eight', 'Livid' or 'Ill Wisher'. In any case the chances of getting a reply to such a missive are remote, and you would have to face some pretty peculiar looks from the postman when he delivered a bundle of mail to 'Mr Livid', 'I. Wisher Esq.' etc.

So I'd advise you to do what I did. I gave birth, quite painlessly, to a retired Colonel, and for a time we were inseparable. We shared the same joys, sorrows and indeed, club. In order not to arouse suspicion,

I deemed it wiser for him to have a residence of his own, and I decided to make him a member of a club. From its safe precincts he could deal with his correspondence and collect the replies. For weeks on end he could be seen scribbling away in the writing room and it was sometimes an embarrassment when I called in at the club post office to ask for my mail.

'No, Commander Bull,' the custodian was apt to reply, 'but there's quite a bit of stuff for your friend Colonel Ironmonger.'

Although most of his early letters contained complaints or adverse comments on policy, our targets increased their range and some of the despatches were of a genial and unprovocative nature. The Colonel started on an interesting investigation into the prevalence of a new type of chiff-chaff that year in Chalfont St Giles, and the astonishing size of vegetable marrows suddenly appearing at Mitcham, which caused a plethora of excited interest among gardening enthusiasts.

Every now and then though the Colonel felt impelled to give a sharp rap over the knuckles to someone or other who provoked him unfavourably by word, thought or deed. If a genuine grievance needed airing he was the first to gird up his loins and strike, whether it was to ameliorate the catering arrangements at some of the London suburban stations, or draw attention to certain irregularities in the conduct of the Wigan branch of the Society for the Prevention of Over-polishing of Dumb Waiters.

One of his favourite hobby horses was dealing with errors of print. A weekly magazine, devoted entirely to the pursuit of pleasure, recklessly announced an Alec Guinness season at one of the Classic Repertory Cinemas. Among the films to be shown were *The Lavender Hill Mob*, 7 March for four days, *The Man in the White Suit*, 11 March for three days, and *Oliver Twist* 14 March for four *years*.

The Colonel felt that he could not let this astonishingly improbable announcement go unchallenged. With a brisk rattle of spurs, he took up his ball-pointed lance and rushed into the lists to face the Editor of the magazine.

Sir,

There seems to be some confusion about the programme of the Classic Cinema, as announced in last week's issue. I rang up the place of entertainment in question to reserve two seats for the film *Oliver Twist* for 23 March 1964. The good lady in the box-office told me she couldn't be certain that this particular film would be showing on this date. Yet I read in your excellent journal that *Oliver Twist* would be at the Classic Cinema for four years, commencing 14 March 1960.

It is really extremely aggravating as I wanted the evening to be a surprise for Mrs Ironmonger, as, by a curious coincidence, the outing would take place exactly ten years after the day on which we got engaged, while we were witnessing this identical film. This auspicious occasion took place at the Camp Theatre in Darjeeling, where I happened to be stationed at the time.

So you can understand that, for sentimental reasons, it is essential to ascertain whether you or the lady supposedly in charge of the arrangements at the Classic Cinema have Right on your side.

Yours etc.,

F. Ironmonger, Lieut-Col. (retired)

Unfortunately the offending magazine paid little attention to this *cri de coeur* and replied shortly but blandly that there had been a printing error. Apparently 'four years' should have read 'four days'. The journal did, however, take the opportunity of wishing the Colonel and his lady every happiness.

Although, as you are sick of hearing, I'm not all that keen on the actual acting, I do like pretending to be somebody else, and to assume someone else's personality in what is called 'real life' attracts me enormously.

That is why it amazes me how cross people get when I have dialled the wrong number in error, or sometimes, I have to admit, as a result of sheer carelessness. From the tone of their voice you would think either (a) that I had done it on purpose, (b) that I was a spy employed by the UnBritish Activities Tribunal or (c) that I was about to say something obscene. The last supposition is the only reasonable one as far as I am concerned, as, not only do I read about that sort of thing in the dear, old-fashioned *News of the World*, but I have been on the receiving end myself. But more of that anon, if not anonymously.

But, you see, I feel totally different if I pick up the receiver and find that someone has dialled *me* by mistake. A fierce sense of exhilaration steals over me and I am instantly transplanted like Walter Mitty into a fantastic and fascinating world. I find myself changing in front of my very own eyes into the person or persons required.

'Is that the Sub-Standard Laundry?' they ask.

'Oh yes, indeed,' I find myself replying with glee, 'and what can I do for you, Sir or Madam?' And immediately I find myself involved in some trauma about missing sheets or torn combinations. I settle their fears by telling them that, though there has been a small fire, their things are perfectly safe. To vary it, sometimes I say that leprosy has broken out among the staff, but it's well under control now, and then the client can relax for the day.

Not only do I spread calm but I also encourage trade.

'Offal is particularly good,' I say to the housewife who has mistaken me for her butcher, 'but I would advise you to pay us an early visit as there is bound to be a run on it.'

I suppose the real reason for my enjoying this kind of lunatic behaviour is that I am a casual labourer and therefore have unlimited time at my disposal. And if by error I do happen to have something important to do, it's lovely to be able to leave it and have a good frivol. (Perfectly good word. The Fowler brothers are mad about it.) As a result the telephone has only to ring once for me to bound across the room to cope with any emergency.

'Is that Reg?'

'Yes,' I say hopefully.

'It doesn't sound like Reg.'

'Well, I've got a bit of a cold,' I parry. But usually they are off the wire before I have found out if they wanted Reg to marry them, give them a thousand pounds, murder their mother or take them to *The Mousetrap*.

Sometimes the caller gets quite cross. I was sitting quiet as a mouse at home one day when the phone went.

'Hello,' I said.

'Hello,' said The Other. 'Is it a black tie or white one?' I thought for a minute.

'I don't really know,' I replied.

'Well it says on the invitation card.'

'Isn't it on yours?' I asked, thinking how clever I was being.

'I've lost mine you idiot,' said the voice, 'that's why I'm ringing you. Go and have a look at yours.'

'OK,' I mumbled. I realized that this might be a genuine conversation stopper. I returned after about three minutes.

'I say, I'm most frightfully sorry,' I said in my best Deb dance voice, 'but I seem to have lost mine too.'

Other End was apoplectic with rage.

'Christ,' it said, 'you might have been quicker'. Then, 'I say, that is Alec isn't it?'

'No,' I said with what I fear amounted to a simper. 'It's Peter as a matter of fact!'

He rang off and a few seconds later the phone went again. I decided to take a chance.

'How do you know we *have* to dress?' I asked. 'It might be a nudist party or Drag.'

I heard a groan from the other end.

'Oh, it's not f—ing you again is it?' and he slammed the receiver down.

But every now and again I find someone willing to play the game my way and an extended and unforeseen conversation with a stranger is not only possible, but can transport one to mysterious realms of fantasy and delight.

For instance I have the good fortune to have a telephone number similar to that of the Classic Cinema Chelsea, so I get involved in some highly risible situations. The other day a lady phoned.

'Can you tell me what you've got on today?' she asked.

'Grey flannels and a rather nice lambswool coat I got off the peg at Harrods' sale,' I replied.

There was a gurgling laugh from the other end of the blower.

'You are *awful*,' the lady said, 'you aren't the Chelsea Classic at all.'

'Well, I'm not actually the Chelsea Classic, but don't hang up because I do happen to know what's on there.'

Silence from the other end and I pursued my advantage.

'It's an early Bardot and the stills outside look jolly sexy, I don't mind telling you.'

'Do they?' she commented severely, and I can't tell you how enchanting she sounded, 'Doubtless you know then what time the film comes on.'

'But of course,' I said. '2, 4, 6, 8, 10. The news is at 1.50, 3.50, 5.50, 7.50, and 9.50. I'll meet you outside at 1.45, 3.45, 5.45, 7.45 or 9.45.'

There was a pause in our conversation. Then,

'The ghastly thing is that I've promised to go with my husband this evening.'

'Make him take you somewhere else,' I said. '*Carry on Scuba Diving* is on at the Odeon.'

'No. I can't. He *loves* the Classic and hates to go anywhere else. But you do sound rather nice.'

'Actually I'm a sex maniac,' I announced, 'but don't let that put you off.'

'It doesn't,' she reassured me, 'but I can't sit here all day waffling to you, pleasant as it's been. Goodbye.'

'No, no. Don't go yet,' I cried at her. 'You must get hold of the right number of the Classic. Got a pencil and paper?'

She had, and there and then I gave her *my* number but she hasn't rung since.

Other diversions to be practised with the help of Mr Alexander Bell's delightful wheeze include finding oneself the third party in a conversation which has been going on happily and undisturbed for some time. One lifts one's own phone for a perfectly legitimate call and finds that a parley is already in full spate. Here, to get the full benefit of this stroke of luck, it is advisable to bide one's time until a suitable moment and then throw in a well-placed comment. This surprises the original participants.

'Did you say something?' they ask one another.

'No I thought it was you.'

'There must be something wrong with the phone.'

'I think he's gone now,' says the more hopeful one. And I remain speechless for a suitable period and then let fly.

Requests ranging from 'Do you mind hanging up? You are on our line,' to the most frightful expletives, some cracking down the phone. Of course I *mind* hanging up. Sometimes I do a very quick click to make them *think* I am no longer there but in fact I remain glued to the receiver and soak in the usually useless bits of information being dished out. A real Listening Tom, that's me. Right at the end I pop in a 'Goodbye. I have so much enjoyed our little chat. Hear from you both again soon, I hope,' which, I would think, unsettles them for the rest of the day.

Sometimes the speakers are so irritating that I can hardly restrain myself. I picked up the phone once and heard a young gent talking to a very South Kensington type of young lady. The conversation was desultory in the extreme. The man was making all the running and the girl was obviously frightfully bored but had nothing else to do. Neither could be classed as a brilliant conversationalist.

'So how did you get home last night?'

'You remember that old Colonel with the gammy leg who would do the Twist?'

'Yes.'

'He drove me home.'

'He didn't!'

'Yes, he did.'

'But he was pissed.'

'Yes, he was a bit. But I couldn't get out of it. He's an old friend of Mummy's. It's my Worst Thing.'

'What is?'

'People being pissed.'

'Yes. It's my Worst Thing, too.'

There was a longish pause. Then the girl thought she must say something.

'How did *you* get home?'

'You remember that big woman in blue? I had to drive her back to Richmond.'

'What was her name?'

'I never found out but I think she arranges flowers for the Queen Mother.'

I thought that was my cue.

'Goodness gracious,' I said, 'that's quite a conversation stopper.' And indeed it was. There was an interim before the girl said, 'Did you say something about a conversation stopper?'

'No, I didn't,' he said.

'I did,' I said.

She said, 'There's someone on the line, I think.' I bided my time and kept quiet while they went on discussing the Mysterious Voice. Then,

'I think they've gone.'

'Yes. So do I.'

'What were you saying before we were interrupted?'

'I can't remember.'

I thought it was time to assist.

'You were talking about the lady who arranged the flowers for the Queen Mother,' I prompted.

'Oh, it's too bad,' said the girl. 'He's on the line again.'

'Let's ignore him,' said her friend. And so they did. They went chuntering on in an aimless fashion until the girl, when asked by the man what she was going to do that weekend, answered,

'I'm going down to Daddy.'

'You're not!' I interposed, deeply shocked. 'How disgusting!' This threw them into a bit of turmoil and I decided to remain mousey quiet until I looked at my watch some ten minutes later.

'Look here,' I broke in on them, 'you've made me late for dinner. It was quite the most boring conversation I've ever heard in my life and I do wish you wouldn't be so thoughtless.' I burst into floods of tears and then put my phone down quietly.

I am bound to admit that I have had my share of anonymous phone calls but only in one case did they have continuity and during the association I found myself turning into a lady called Phyllis.

It all started as a result of a conversation with my 'daily' whom I found purse-lipped when I returned from a shopping spree.

'Mr Bull, I think you ought to get on to Scotland Yard at once,' she announced.

'Why, Mrs Pye?' I asked. 'Have we been burgled?'

'No, sir, but there's been this terrible man on the phone saying horrible things.'

'What sort of things?' I asked, thrilled to the marrow.

'Oh, sir, I couldn't bring myself to tell *you*, sir, but it was all about knickers and measurements,' she said darkly.

'Leave it to me, Mrs Pye,' I said, trying desperately to recall whether one had to dial 100 instead of 999, as one seems to have to do now for everything.

But, what with lunch and the washing-up I forgot all about it until later in the day, when the phone rang several times in fairly quick succession. I kept on picking up the bloody thing and saying 'Hello' cordially, but all the reply I got was some rather asthmatic breathing, and the click of a replaced instrument. It was not a highly satisfactory form of intercourse, and was nothing to do with the Generation Gap. I realized that I was dealing with what is described in the courts as a Breacher of the Peace.

It must be pointed out before we go further or indeed too far, that I was at this time living in a flat recently vacated by a charming actress, whose name had remained in the telephone directory long after she'd left the building. Her engagement had just been announced in *The Times* and other newspapers, and these two combined facts were responsible for the confusion which was to engulf me for the next few weeks or so.

Anyhow, the next time the phone rang I decided to teach the caller a tiny lesson. I answered him in a ladylike way. This caused my unknown communicator to open his trap for the first time. He asked me if I was Phyllis. I admitted that it was indeed my name. He then went straight into the attack. Did my fiancé know I was not a virgin and that he (the caller) had had me innumerable times? I simulated outrage in a high falsetto, which is frightfully tiring, and then he proceeded to make about ten not frightfully old-fashioned suggestions about what he'd like to do to me, or rather dear old Phyllis.

It would be hypocritical to pretend that I was remotely shocked. I found it, I have to admit, rather erotic and jokey to a degree. I let him prattle on happily, every now and then throwing in an 'Oh but you mustn't say things like that!' or 'Stop it! You're disgusting.' Anyhow, he finally rang off, obviously deeply satisfied, and that was that.

Well it wasn't as a matter of fact. He was on the blower frequently and was so persistent that I thought out a plan to Teach Him A Lesson. Such was his ardour that I was convinced that I might be able to entice him round to see me in person. Little fool that I was! I didn't realize then that the only thrill these kind of people (sneer! sneer!) get out of it is the fact that they can't be seen and can *imagine* their effect on the person they are persecuting. In those days I was nowhere near as sophisticated in these matters as I am now, so I thought that it was up to me to keep him on a string, or in this case a bit of tangled cord. At the right moment I would issue an invitation and then, when he rang my bell (front door), I'd be there and usher him in, saying graciously,

'I'm Phyllis. Do come in. It's so nice to *see* you and not hear you for a change.'

After carefully closing the door to prevent his flight I'd introduce him to the small but select audience whom I would have assembled there.

But he proved difficult to pin down and for over two weeks my life was turned upside down. What with answering everyone, including my aged mother and my agent (no, they're not the same person, you fool!) in a falsetto voice, there was complete disruption in the home, not helped by my more tasteless friends ringing up pretending to be what Mr Tennessee Williams might describe as my Gentleman Caller.

Some of the ordinary people who phoned me during this period hurriedly put the phone down, thinking I'd either had a disastrous accident or gone potty, and any prospective employers were frightened away. Things couldn't go on like this as none of our nerves would stand it. I decided it had gone far enough.

At a particularly unsuitable moment during the night, the blower went and My Caller asked me if I'd had my bath and was I wearing anything under my housecoat? For some reason he was mad about housecoats. I replied in a falsetto that I wasn't even wearing a housecoat, which sent him, I imagine, into a frenzy of excitement.

'Oh,' he said, 'haven't you had your bath yet?'

'As a matter of fact,' I replied, 'I haven't. In any case I'm going to shave first.'

There was a gasp from the other end of the blower.

'So sucks to you,' I said, speaking in my normal voice. 'And double sucks,' I said in a falsetto.

I heard a groan and that was the end of this not frightfully savoury episode. All rather sad, really.

14
Well, I'll be Muggered

No one could accuse me of being trendy, yet medically I seem to be following the pace-setters. I had my appendix out just as a number of film stars were embarking on a similar operation, I got phlebitis just after a president or three was suffering from same and I currently am recovering from the results of being mugged in dear old London town. Employees of London Transport and Mr Charles Bronson in the kinematograph *Death Wish* have my sympathy in our mutual plights.

There were two ironical undertones to the incident which I am about to describe. Firstly I had just clocked in from New York where all the inhabitants, including resident aliens like myself, are used to this sort of thing and proceed warily all the time. I know I manage always to sit next to one of the fairly friendly cops who patrol the subway train carriages. And in the streets I trot round like a very fat fox who suspects that he is being followed by a pack of extremely athletic hounds who are what is known as 'hot on the scent'.

The other coincidence was that I had just been dining with my beloved medical adviser, who, in his customary sneaky way, had served a delicious repast and, as I was leaving, had insisted on taking my blood pressure. 'Not good, far too high,' he muttered. 'You must avoid all excitement and stress.' A few minutes later, when I found myself flat on my back in a street near Victoria Station fighting for what was literally dear life, I did not have the opportunity to follow his instructions to the letter.

I was accompanied on the expedition by my partner, Don Busby, an American chap, who with the help of my services as assistant mailing department *and* tea lady, runs Zodiac, The Astrological Emporium (Notting Hill Gate end of Kensington Church Street, Advt). Honestly and truthfully, I only dish out this info because, as a result of our venture, I have become very conscious of that maddening phrase, 'What will be, will be' or, as Miss Doris Day put it, 'Que sera, sera'. To put things clearer, I am pointing out that the whole unpleasant episode under survey might have been foreseen in my palm, tarot cards or birth chart.

A year ago a clairvoyant, Kathy McCormack by name, whom I had not met before, warned me of 'great danger from a floor or ceiling'. As she had been remarkably accurate throughout her tarot-card reading, I took note. The next day I asked the lodger to help me move the refrigerator and roll the linoleum back. He promptly fell straight through the floor to the bedroom below. Luckily he clutched me, thus breaking his fall. Actually we knew we had a bit of dry rot but this was beyond a joke. If we'd waited, there is little doubt that the following week the fridge would have descended to the floor below, accompanied by the writer of this article and it's anybody's guess as to which would have arrived on top of the other.

Georgina, our resident palmist, has just issued a pronunciamento about a dicey staircase in my flat and frightened the daylights out of me. Nowadays, when I eat with her, I sit with my palms huddled over the fodder to ensure that she can't find a reason to hint at future disasters. I only want to hear about lovely future happenings, like winning the Pools and/or the fashion competition in the *News of the World*. I enter the latter hopefully every week trusting I will repeat my 1951 triumph when I successfully forecast a lot of blouses in order of popularity.

However, even if astrology, etc. is a large part of my business, one can carry ESP too far. When a crystal ball fell on my head recently while I was doing the light dusting, it was in my opinion silly of people to tell me that I should have looked into the bloody thing the day before and then I would have foreseen the accident. And a fat lot of good *that* would have done me.

But to return to the nasty occurrence. Mr Busby and I left our doctor's house in Pimlico and started to make our way towards

Victoria. It was a Friday night, the pubs had just emptied and the streets were full, a fact which I'd ask you to bear in mind.

In Wilton Road we passed three gentlemen who made some disparaging remark as we came abreast of them. We paid no attention and a few seconds later we found ourselves doubled up on the ground being bashed and kicked to bits. Luckily Mr B. is as strong as a horse and delivered some smartish blows to the groins of our attackers. No one in the vicinity made any attempt to interfere but the chaps finally left us. Bleeding and shaken we picked ourselves up and proceeded on our way, but, looking over my shoulder, I caught sight of our assailants pursuing us. Coming up on our right was a smartish restaurant with a little terrace. Don suggested that we should take refuge there and instructed me to run for it, while he protected me from another onslaught. I didn't quite make it in time and once again we both found ourselves on the ground and this time our enemies had armed themselves with dustbin lids. However, by superhuman efforts, we managed to get up and inside the restaurant.

We were met by the manager who didn't seem best pleased to see us and, instead of showing us to a table, ordered us to leave immediately. Although we were both bleeding profusely, we still didn't look like drunken yobs, or indeed sound like them. Or so we thought. The waiters meanwhile held and locked the front door and managed to keep out the *Clockwork Orange* figures who were, as we realized later, either drunk or stoned out of their minds. I shall remember the looks of hate on their horrible faces until the day I die.

Inside the restaurant to the right there was one party of twelve who were the only customers. 'You must leave at once,' repeated the manager to us, 'I have a very distinguished clientele.' I turned to the very distinguished clientele and asked it to forgive our precipitous and untidy entrance. One of the men at the table said that none of them wanted to get involved and they continued to tuck into their dinner, which I hope included a powdered-glass soufflé.

I had sat down to catch my breath and steady myself at a table but the manager soon stopped that. 'I shall call the police if you don't go at once,' he shouted. 'That is just what we would like you to do,' said

Mr Busby quietly. 'Come this way,' ordered mine host. We followed him with docility to what he indicated as his office. It turned out to be the gents' loo, into which he tried to lock us. Showing some unexpected spirit we refused this type of refuge and he pushed us further into the building. I think both Don and I were both by now so stunned that we didn't realize where he was taking us. The fact remains that we found ourselves *outside* the restaurant and in an alley which led into the main thoroughfare where we suspected the thugs might still be lurking. The manager had locked the door behind us and we felt trapped.

We stood motionless and silent for what seemed like hours. Finally Don crept down cautiously to the street. After a brief survey of the situation he beckoned me to follow. There was no sign of our assailants but suddenly there was a screech of sirens and a small fleet of police cars drew up in front of us. After brief questioning, two cars left to search for the muggers but, as it turned out, never caught up with them. We were left with a rather lethargic copper who asked us our ages, professions and addresses. We couldn't make out how the police had got wind of the affair until a good samaritan arrived on the scene. With his wife in a flat opposite, he had watched the entire distressing scene and phoned 999.

He gave a far more coherent description of our attackers than we were able to do. After being thanked for his solicitude, he returned to his home, which is just what we longed to do. Return to our homes, I mean. We asked the policeman to get us a taxi but he waved airily in the direction of the station and told us we'd find one around there easily enough. I pointed out that we didn't at the moment look like a good passenger risk but even this didn't move him into action. We started walking shakily northwards.

Our first bit of luck that evening, apart from the lovely dinner and not being actually killed, came up in the shape of a coloured driver who, after a cursory look at our disarray, told us to hop in, which we gladly did. I dropped my partner off at his Fulham Road flat and went on to my temporary accommodation in Holland Park (temporary owing to the aforementioned collapsed ceiling). As I descended from his taxi, the driver said, 'Excuse me, sir, but aren't you on the films?'

'Not tonight,' I replied (wrily seems to be the correct adverb) and made for my bed.

Funnily enough we didn't feel the full impact of the incident immediately. The day after it we stood behind the counter of the Emporium showing our war wounds unattractively but proudly. However, on the Sunday I did crack up and for about a week couldn't talk about the affair without bursting into floods of tears, which must have embarrassed my long-suffering but loyal friends. I think I was in a state of shock, but not so much at the violent and totally unprovoked attack. (It is interesting to note that nothing was stolen. A pendant was wrenched from my partner's neck but our wallets remained untouched.) No, it was the behaviour of the people in the street and that restaurant which horrified me. The name of the latter I will divulge on the receipt of an SAE. (The food may be lovely.)

I was also alerted to the depressing fact that now in London we must be as wary as everyone is in New York and Detroit. Our own personal awareness has made us almost paranoid. On Saturday nights, when we deposit the loot in one of those vaults outside the bank, we accompany each other like a couple of gangsters with guns at the ready. In the shop we keep a bottle of Ajax spray handy by the counter.

The other day our medical adviser asked us to dine again. 'What time shall we approach?' I asked. 'Oh,' he replied, 'I've got the decorators in so just wander round about 8.30.' I didn't like to spread alarm and despondency to the dear man but the one thing we were determined never to do in that particular area was to 'wander around'. We decided to take a taxi-cabriolet and blow the expense.

Goodness, how sad.

15
Look to the Stars

As readers of *Tit Bits, Harper's Bazaar, Screw* magazine, *Vogue,* the *Kensington Post, Reveille* and TV viewers of 'The David Dimbleby Talk-In' have realized, with my sincere gratitude to these institutions, I am now a partner in an Astrological Emporium called 'Zodiac' at the Notting Hill Gate end of Kensington Church St. I suppose I've always wanted to play at shops since I was about six years old, and it is fortunate that in the 'tea-time of life' as my father called it, I have been able to realize my dream. Luckily my partner, Don Busby, doesn't 'Play at it' otherwise I think we would be out of business by now.

Originally I wanted to combine it with some Gipsy Tea Rooms and who knows but that I won't again strike lucky and, handsomely attired and backed up by a small ladies' band, be dispensing crumpets and raspberry jam, anchovy toast and home-made cakes to all and sundry. Particularly sundry. Thrown in will be a first-class tea-cup reading by our staff ('resting' actors and actresses thinly disguised as wandering gipsies). I think this is just what London is clamouring for. Mark you, I think people will be so mad about the idea that there will be a danger of them outstaying their welcome in which case I shall have parking meters by the tables so that the occupants can stay as long as they like if they pay extra.

But all this will have to wait until I can find proper premises. The snag all along has been that it is almost impossible to get a brand new 'Catering Licence' for premises which haven't had it before, and it has been impossible to persuade local councils that there will be no cooking, except of accounts and crumpets. 'Ah,' but they expostulate, 'how do we know that you won't turn into a fish and chips shop?' I tell them in a haughty voice that it is extremely unlikely and keep on thinking of the way Beatrice Lillie says 'Me,wot's always 'ad me own 'orses'. So that's that. When we came across this little building in Kensington Mall we knew it was right to buy it. There was a Teddy Bear in the corner of the top room, for starters. The whole place was in the peak of condition and as pretty as paint. The people who owned it were dears. They asked a lot, we agreed and, compared with the sort of stuff we had been seeing, it was a bargain.

For several months we'd been on the search and were 'gazumped' out of a building in Pimlico Road, on which we'd rather set our hearts. But it was possibly a stroke of luck that it happened, as our current home has a happier atmosphere about it and is ideal for the purpose. If only you could have seen some of the premises we were offered. Even the Estate Agents reeled back at the pong as we entered a lot of them. They obviously had never set foot in them and the floor was littered with bills for the last four tenants; one would never have had a quiet moment, what with the drains, and the writ-servers outnumbering the customers by at least two to one.

We were originally thinking of letting the flat upstairs to Russian spies as I got rather windy when we thought of how much we owed the bank. Also it'd be fun when they were arrested (it's v. near the Embassy) to say, 'They were just ordinary people like you and me,' to the reporters. But if we did this we realized that (a) we should have to put a loo in the shop below, because of Staff Regulations Article 2384 or something, (b) we would have to hire one of the garages opposite for extra storage and (c) we would never be able to cook anything for ourselves. So we live above the premises on and off and it's all very cosy with Georgina, our palmist, in a room on the first floor, about whom more anon.

It's only since our brave decision that we've also found out that, if we *had* let the flat above there would have been nowhere to sit down and the whole thing would have been hell. Quite apart from having to put bugging devices into the flat to catch the Russian spies at it, if you know what I mean. So now we've got the best of both possible worlds, a thing I always think very worthwhile.

Mark you, I couldn't have undertaken the shop without D. Busby, who is a Leo and as tough as old boots. It was he who calmly announced many months before we had opened or even found premises, that he was off to Blackpool. As he had never been north of Golders Green before I was impressed. 'Why?' I asked. 'The Blackpool Gift Fair,' he announced. 'Of course,' I said, having never heard of the thing. So off he trotted, spent three days there, commuting from Manchester as Blackpool was full of the 20,000 traders who visit it at that time of year and back he came with assorted specimens, all to do with the Zodiac. He accumulated stock like a squirrel nuts and it was fascinating watching an American make himself quite so much at home in our grey and fairly pleasant land.

As I was still, and in a way still am, planning the Gipsy Tea Rooms, I let him run the shop. I am treated as a sort of cretinous tea lady and when I'm the Mailing Department, which is quite often, I am not really trusted to do up a Fortune Tea Cup (60p plus 17p for postage and a bargain at that), but I love dealing with the actual mail. It's fun to me to bring back courtesy into relationships with customers. I start off letters with 'Your esteemed order' or 'Your kind enquiry' and end up 'Assuring you of our best attention always, I remain your obedient servant' which, I imagine, hits them between the eyes. I know sudden politeness, like a bus actually stopping at a Request Stop when one holds up one's hand, or somebody holding a door open for me in Boots the Cash Chemists, is apt to reduce me to tears. Anyhow Courtesy is our Watchword. And, as for the customers who come into the shop, let them wander round as long as they like. Let them read whole books, as long as they don't break the backs of same, feel all the Tarot cards etc. and then not buy anything, with a sweet smile we say 'Thank You' as they leave the building in such a way that either they return forthwith or break their bloody necks on the step out of sheer surprise.

Oh yes, I'm very keen on proving that I come from a nation of shopkeepers and am getting pretty ruthless at the job. Don't think I don't fill all the Zodiac piggy-banks with a half p so that the children can hear them rattle. The other day a patently rich lady brought her very difficult six-year old in to 'buy a present for Daddy'. She kept on, to our delight, showing him the more expensive gifts. The kiddiwink expressed extreme boredom and thumbed down the lot. I slid along with some of our most expensive crystal goblets. 'Do you think,' I said to the child in my most cooing voice, 'Daddy would like this for his toothbrush?' And that was six quid in the kitty without much pain. Oh I do hope this isn't putting you off visiting our shop.

Everyone asks me how we came to think of it. After all it's the first shop of its kind in Britain. And I don't know if my answer is satisfactory enough. Some years ago, I was given by Mr and Mrs André Morell (Joan Greenwood to you) a most lovely black and gold Portmerion mug. It was in Aries natch (as I happen to have been born on the First Day of Spring) and the thing was that I was shortly leaving for America and I couldn't think of anything I'd really like to take more as presents for my friends. Leo and Capricorn were what I lusted after and could I find them at any of the stores who stocked these particular mugs? Not on your nelly! Can that last phrase be right? It looks peculiar from where I'm sitting.

Anyhow my friends had to go without that visit but when Don Busby came over from the States to live and we were playing about with the idea of an Astrology shop, I did think it would be rather nice if we could have a complete stock of every sign. Now then, don't all come rushing along the moment you read this because my theory had one fatal flaw. No, two. Transport and availability of material. We order crystal eggs from Sweden and the damned things lie about in docks for months and in Britain work on crystal glass was practically suspended for several months except for goods which featured the silver wedding of Our Gracious Queen. Another astonishing factor is that there is no doubt that certain signs sell better than others. Virgo people have a reputation for being 'picky' (they would describe themselves as perfectionists) so we don't sell as many of them. No Cancerian is v. keen on their sign and Scorpio people are impulsive and prefer the glyph of their sign on jewellery rather than the actual animal. My dears, the things I've learned since the shop opened.

Aries persons (like me) keep on hitting their heads and it is absolutely true. My partner, Mr Busby, can spot them practically before they have gone round the shop, because of their impulsive behaviour. It's the same with handwriting. We have some rather chic visitors' books upstairs where our friends sign their names and put their date of birth (not year as the ladies aren't all that keen, to say nothing of some of the gents). You'd be *amazed* at the results, when you view a whole page of these Visiting Sheets. Aries write very small and Sagittarians very big and seem to be colossal show-offs (they write messages in Greek or Hebrew and that sort of thing). The Cancer lot follow the spacing of the person above, exactly like sheep, whereas the Librans *have* to balance things, and, if there is an empty space on a page, they leap in there. Scorpios have flashy signatures with big capitals and Taurus handwriting is firm and stolid.

Now I've noticeably got less and less sceptical since we opened and, I assure you, it's not for financial (or even publicity) reasons. You see, so many extraordinary things have happened. For instance the lady wot does horoscopes who suddenly came into our lives. I came bouncing into the shop one morning and this lady hands me My Natal Chart. And for those of you who know nothing about the subject, an NC is a geometrical expression of the planetary tendencies at the time you were born. In order to make it valid, the exact time and place are required, as longitude and latitude have to be allowed for in calculations.

So I thanked the nice lady and asked her how the hell she knew when I was born.

'It's on page one of *Bulls in the Meadows*,' she replied sweetly. And that *was* a conversation stopper. A few days later she sent me my entire horoscope. It was extremely well observed and there were conclusions drawn, for which she could not have had a clue. I called her up to thank her. Her name is Joyce Sanderson by the way. She then announced that she'd done a horoscope of the shop. I did chortle a bit at that one and got a well-deserved rebuke from the other end of the blower.

'If you know the date of birth of a seemingly inanimate object, it's perfectly easy to plan a chart for it,' she said severely. 'Why on earth did you open on 1 May? All the signs were against it. Did something dreadful happen that day?'

I had to admit that the sign-writer hadn't finished his work by the time we opened and a ladder was firmly poised against the front door for the whole of the morning. This kept the superstitious customers away. However Joyce assured me that 'Zodiac's' dear little chart showed an unbroken line of success from that moment on except for one thing. I asked her what.

It seemed that there was danger of fire. At this I nearly dropped the phone. The day before there had been a fire at the back of the shop next door and I'd had to call the fire brigade. As Joyce lives in Essex she couldn't have seen it or indeed heard of it but our building was slightly singed and I bought a fire extinguisher next day. But it's the combination of coincidences which is too strong to ignore. If I started telling you of some of our palmist's successes you wouldn't believe them. And it's not that she told us (palmists take a kind of hippocratic oath like doctors) but her clients would come whirring down from her room amazed and bewildered by her ESP – the conjuring up of an exact portrait of a loved one or an aspect of a career about which only the client knew.

She has been a great asset to the shop and it is fascinating to me the way you can always tell the people who are sceptical and yet want a go. They shuffle round the shop pretending to look at the books and other goods, but waiting for the shop to be empty. Then there is usually this conversation:

'Do you believe in all this sort of stuff?'

'As a matter of fact I do,' I reply.

'Oh, I don't. I think it's all a lot of codswallop, rubbish, balls' (according to the type of speaker).

Silence.

'*You* don't believe in this palmist stuff do you?'

'Yes.'

'Extraordinary.' Fingering of the palmist's card goes on.

'Well I don't. But she isn't by chance free now, is she? You see I've got this problem and, though I've made up my mind, I'd like a second opinion.' And that's that. They're hooked on it and in nine cases out of ten, they come down beaming and contented.

We also have attached to us an Astrologer, a Graphologist, a Tarot Card reader, quite apart from dear Mrs Sanderson, who has appointed herself Court Consultant and won't take a penny for all the work she puts in, settling our future hashes.

Not content with starting on an astrological career, I have also got involved in the Ladies' Literary Lunch circuit.

Whereas I've practically had to give up acting owing to nerves and the general tension which surrounds the world of entertainment nowadays, I don't mind the improvised part of it all. I don't mean I like pretending I am a tree or a piece of parsley, I mean it's not difficult for me to say the first words which come into my head. Whereas proper actors hate the TV-talk shows and it scares the daylights out of them even to open a bazaar, I really rather thrive on that sort of thing and, when Cyril Fletcher asked me if I'd like to become part of his circus called 'Associated Speakers', I said yes with alacrity before he changed his mind.

Now all you have to do to be an Associated Speaker is to get up fairly early in the morning from time to time and take a railway train out of London to some other city. The clubs pay your first-class fare and so it's a question of whipping into the loo with your second-class ticket just before arrival at your destination and pocketing the extra money later, when your cheque is discreetly handed to you. The loo deception is just in case the secretary of the club is bold enough to come on the platform. One of the secretaries did try and fob me off with second-class expenses on the grounds that I was a friend of her son's. I told her, through Associated Speakers, that it was unlikely that I would remain his friend, if I didn't get my first-class ticket. So *that* was all right.

On arrival at your destination you are met by the secretary of the club or one of her deputies and usually driven straight to the rendezvous where, at first sight, the room seems just full of hats. One has sort of forgotten that people wear hats any more but Ladies' Literary Lunches are massed with them. If one is too early one is given a whirl round the town and shown the sights and very interesting that can be. On one occasion I was taken to a coffee Klatch of ladies, where I was introduced to the Lady Mayoress, who greeted me with the words:

'Oh I'm so relieved it's you! I thought you were going to be a Chinese lady.'

I was a little startled by this until the secretary replied:

'No, Lady Mayoress, that's next month, when we have Ying Si-fong telling us about Flower Decoration. This is Mr Bull, who has come to talk to us about Teddy Bears.'

But soon it's time for lunch, which is usually pretty ropey (there have been notable exceptions like Newark but that was a notable visit throughout), and sharp at two o'clock I am on my feet. I am practically always introduced by Madam Chairman who can be wildly disconcerting with remarks like:

'Did you *really* get the DSC?' or 'You won't be too long will you, Mr Bull, because most of the ladies have their bridge at 3.30.' On one occasion I didn't like to say that I'd already set my sights on catching the 3.19 out of the city.

My lecture, as it's so flatteringly called, lasts about forty minutes, with five minutes for questions. Unlike most speakers I vary it a great deal according to the look of my audience, before I get to my feet. At the first yawn I tend to say something so outrageous or unexpected that those about to have a zizz pull themselves together, but I'm afraid most of them don't mind who talks to them, as long as they are talked *at*. If I can't hold them with Teddy Bears I switch to my Greek House or vice versa. But they are mostly pretty good, though I don't envy the secretaries who have to engage us and deal with complaints. I gather that speakers are critized mainly for dress. 'She looked so dowdy, considering . . .' or 'My dear, did you see? He had frayed cuffs.' I actually overheard the latter, just before I was about to get to my feet. They weren't talking about me but it did so happen that my zip had broken that morning so I wasn't exactly sitting or rather standing pretty. The speed with which I sat down and stood up must have surprised a good many of my audience. I resembled a rather plump jack in the box.

Once a year there is an excruciatingly droll ceremony at the Dorchester Hotel where we all pay a great deal for our lunches and meet our opposite numbers, the Secretaries and Madam Chairwomen, I mean Mesdames Chairwomen, bearing on their breasts the name of their club. Here they march round and give us (our names are clearly visible) the once over. And it's just that. I remember being slightly disconcerted when a couple of prospective employers came right up to me, studied my badge and one said to the other, 'Peter Bull,' and the other said, 'Yes, we *thought* of having him but we didn't.'

Later one goes into lunch to a vast room which stretches for miles. At the centre table are all the big knobs of the Associated Speaking world, flanking Mr and Mrs Cyril Fletcher (Miss Betty Astell to you and me). The smaller fry are dispersed at various tables and I was fortunate enough to be at the table of the new double-barrelled secretary of the Jersey Luncheon Club, who didn't actually engage me on the spot but was plainly as nervous as I and equally bewildered. It was both our christenings in this particular battlefield. After a lunch of which I can remember little, except that there seemed to be a lot of peas, came the speeches. Mr Fletcher made a welcoming one, with wit and tact, and then the fun began. Lady Barnett thanked Mr Fletcher on behalf of the guests and both sides were asked to voice any complaints. A mild lady on behalf of the clubs said it would be a help if speakers engaged and unable to fulfil the appointment could give plenty of warning. For the Speakers the Duke of Bedford got up and complained that there was far too much talk about local matters before he was allowed to speak. He implied that he had come to Speak and not listen to whose marrow had won the Women's Institute competition.

It was at this moment that I thought that all the Secretaries and Chairwomen who annually paid vast sums to hear His Grace Speak might rise in a body and string him up to a lamp-post outside the dear old Dorchester. However A.N. Other got up and said that he couldn't disagree more with the Duke and was delighted to hear all the local news and that was almost the nicest thing about travelling round lecturing. I could see thousands of pencils working overtime and I don't think A.N. Other need worry about his bread and butter, to say nothing of jam, for several seasons. A lady got up and said calmly and without malice and anger that she had had only one booking the whole season and wasn't it possible for anyone who wasn't a TV personality to interest the clubs? There was a lot of shuffling of feet at that. My godson, Sheridan Morley, relieved the tension by getting up to complain that it would be nice if he wasn't always greeted with the phrase, 'Oh you're much fatter than you look on the telly!' After him there was a good deal of waffling and I left the building fairly quietly. As I was getting my coat, Mr Harry Wheatcroft presented me with a red rose or three, which was the kindliest gesture of the whole occasion.

I don't think I shall go next year and maybe the novelty of the whole merry-go-round will have worn off by then. At the back of my mind I feel it's all a dress rehearsal for a lecture tour in America where the financial rewards are tremendous. My agent over there tells me that I can expect to get $850 per talk and a month of that per year would suit me fine. He is however trying to persuade me to make it a whole evening which worries me somewhat. He has suggested that I should include theatrical readings and heaven knows what else, so I suppose it's back to my long speech from *Luther* and dear old Sergeant Buzfuz. He has however suggested the ideal title for such a disastrous-seeming enterprise.

'An Evening of Bull'. Well we shall see, shan't we?

16
Bear Necessities

The Ministry of Pensions, my family, and even I myself, can now relax regarding the problems attending my fast-approaching old age.

The change in attitude has been wrought about quite simply by realizing that my Teddy Bears have suddenly pulled themselves together and gone out to work – in order, I imagine, to allow me to continue to go on living in the style to which I have been accustomed. I have long been conscious of their general therapeutic powers but have only just gauged their earning potential and consequent relief to my financial angst.

Let me explain before your bile rises to boiling point: Granada Television was casting Evelyn Waugh's *Brideshead Revisited*, an ambitious production involving many months of filming. An important character in the book is Aloysius, a teddy bear belonging to Lord Sebastian Flyte, one of the anti-heroes of the story. The producer, Derek Granger, approached me about supplying an actor for the role. I immediately thought of Delicatessan, a distinguished example of vintage bear, who had been able to observe every facet of life from a shelf in a grocery store in Maine, where he reposed for fifty years. His owner, a Miss Euphemia Ladd, had decided to give up her shop and thought her furry friend needed a change. She'd seen my little lot on American TV and asked if they and I would look after Delicatessen.

We said yes but of course, and he arrived in a large cardboard box. Far from enjoying a well-deserved retirement, he has now made himself indispensable to a curious entertainment called *An Evening of Bull* which I am apt to do in places like Lexington, Kentucky, or

Hastings, Sussex. The *soi-disant* show opens with him sitting on a chair with a spotlight on his dear old face and we bow to each other from time to time, to give us both confidence.

So he went off for his audition for the role of Aloysius with a certain amount of stage experience and secured it against all comers, including the resident ted at Castle Howard, where a lot of the filming took place. The latter was reported to be a bit miffed and abruptly turned down the job of stand-in. It had been deemed wiser that Delicatessen should not be exposed to the rigours of a fast ride in an automobile and other hazards. A contract was dished out, but as yet he is not a fully fledged member of Equity. It was decided, however, that he should be referred to throughout as 'the artist' and not 'the property', though officially he was the responsibility of the property department.

During the long drawn-out strike, he didn't shirk his responsibilities and could be observed on the picket line in Golden Square, carrying a banner which read 'ITV Unfair to Bears'. Mr Granger assured me he was well and happy and eligible for relief from the ACTT Hardship Fund, if necessary.

He resumed work after the strike and all went smoothly until I wanted him back for a recent US tour. I called Mr G. on the blower-machine. There was a shocked silence. Then: 'But you can't jeopardize your client's career at this critical juncture.'

'What *do* you mean?' I asked.

'He's due to go to Venice on Thursday with Lord Olivier.'

That did it. I could already see the entry in the *Spotlight* casting directory: 'Recently co-starring with Laurence Olivier in *Brideshead Revisited*.' Offers would come pouring in and we'd both have to be registered for VAT. I began to regret the enforced retirement of Dusty, another Thespian ted, whom I had rescued from a dustbin and who is not to be confused with Miss Dusty Springfield's egg-head bear, who is actually called Mr Einstein.

Dusty played an important part in an unsuccessful musical called *The Tiger and the Lady*. Still, he got a nice notice in *The Times*, which he carried on the wrist of his paw, attached by an elastic band. I was warned, before he accepted the engagement, that the part involved being thrown about the stage a bit. He told me he didn't mind and admitted to a masochistic streak, owing to his recent confinement to the dustbin, which he'd rather enjoyed as he hoped that this experience might land him a job in one of Mr Samuel Beckett's plays.

He now lives in the lap of luxury with a Mr Kenneth More, who, I was told on extremely reliable authority, had never possessed a teddy and consequently felt deprived. Dusty and Mr More got together at Christmas and doubtless he will be put up for the Garrick Club and I can only hope that he doesn't get blackballed.

But, quite seriously, the therapeutic powers of the teddy bear have now started to be acknowledged even in medical circles and twice I have been asked to deliver lectures to postgraduate doctors on the subject. On one of these occasions the gent who was in charge called me on the blower and asked if I was bringing my slides. This threw me into a temporary tizzy but on recovering I replied that I would be bringing case histories in letter form and some bears who would speak for themselves.

The material I have amassed on the subject is quite astonishing. Teddies carried as totems by Battle of Britain pilots, a Mr Woppit who helped Donald Campbell break every record on land and sea, another bear who gave an alpine climber the courage to reach the top of the Matterhorn, and masses who have comforted the lonely, the bereaved, and the invalids. They've even been known to save lives and a notable case which received vast newspaper coverage was that of young Mark Wallis. Knocked over by a lorry, he was taken to hospital where he lay in a coma for two days. On the third day his frantic mother left his bedside and fetched his beloved teddy and laid it so that it touched his hand. In a few minutes a finger moved and then another and the feel of the accustomed fur speeded a miraculous recovery.

There is now an excellent organization called Good Bears of the World, which supplies teddies to hospitals, to be given to children on that first rather frightening night. For a small sum you can join GBW (as it's called) and get a quarterly magazine, *Bear Tracks*, which reports on teddy news from all over the globe.

The Great TB Rally at Longleat in 1979 attracted just over 50,000 of them, bringing 20,000 humans. And I'm here to tell you the average age of the visitors was nearer forty than fourteen. There was a similar function in Sydney and I sent my largest bear to represent Britain. He went out first class and returned likewise, much too pleased with himself and wearing a not entirely suitable silver Qantas T-shirt. Next year my special friend Theodore (who has been with me bear and cub for forty years) and I have been invited to the second Australian rally and doubtless my companion will get all the attention and fringe benefits.

Meantime, to be practical, I've opened a Post Office Savings account for Delicatessen though I have had to change his name by deed poll (it was in *The Times*) to Aloysius so that he can cash in on the inevitable burst of publicity when his *magnum opus* reaches your screens. I gather he is already a subscriber to a press-cutting bureau and I must remember to get him to draw up his will as quickly as possible.

17
The Summing Up

I love the majority of my fellow-actors immoderately, but I am the first to admit that they can be infuriating, puerile and, on occasions, as intelligent as moths. It is when they start discussing their careers and their agents that claustrophobia and irritation set in with me. The theme 'My Agent' is a conversational must, whenever two actors on amicable but not intimate terms meet.

'My Agent is the most iniquitous, most wonderful, wickedest, sharpest, slowest, laziest, crookedest, silliest, cleverest, best, worst in London'; I have never heard anyone talking about their agents except in superlatives, and I don't think I remember any actor just saying that they had a satisfactory agent.

'I can't imagine why I employ an agent,' is a phrase used pretty non-stop.

I know exactly why I employ one, and I don't envy any of the twenty-odd ladies and gents who have tried to sell me to prospective employers over the years. I certainly don't grudge them the ten per cent which they get for handling what might be larkily called 'my business'. I would rather (only don't tell them) give them twenty per cent than discuss terms myself. As to fixing 'the billing', the mere idea of it gives me the shudders and in most cases I prefer to remain anonymous; unlike the star who was caught outside a West-End theatre, measuring the posters with a foot-rule, to see if his name took up more space than that of his co-star.

Another conversational waste of time with actors is discussing what photograph they are to insert in *Spotlight* (the actor's catalogue of wares for casting purposes). Your friend brings round a pile of pictures, showing him or herself in various clothes, make-ups, poses and hair-dos. You wade religiously through them and eventually choose one which you like.

'Do you think so? Funny,' is your friend's only comment. You choose another.

'Um,' says your friend. 'Charles liked that one. I think it's awful.' At the end of two hours they disappear, oozing gratitude and saying you have saved their life; and a totally different photograph from any you have liked appears in the next issue of *Spotlight*.

Another curious trait that most actors (including myself) possess is a total inability to understand why friends sometimes don't come round backstage after a performance. This invariably leads to unpleasantness of some sort.

'He, she or they can't have liked me, us or it.'

'Extraordinary behaviour not coming round.'

'Peter, Sybil, John or Jeanette have changed since they got into that TV quiz game,' and so on.

What we never seem to realize is that their non-appearance after the show was due to the fact that either (a) they were with someone who had an epileptic fit and had to be taken home during the show, or (b) they had only limited time to catch their train to Guildford, or (c) they had loathed every second of it and hesitated to come round and say so, or (d) they had been so moved that they were going straight home to write a fan letter, or (e) they had just finished an affair with another member of the company and didn't want to run the risk of running into him or her backstage, or (f) they didn't know we knew they were in front and hated going round anyhow.

I personally dislike going backstage intensely. I find I am absolutely tongue-tied and unable to express my pleasure if I *have* loved it and incapable of saying, 'It's wonderful,' if I've had an unenjoyable evening. I can now, with age, no longer even bring myself to say, 'It's been a most interesting evening,' which used to be my stand-by conversational gambit on these occasions. For these reasons I try to avoid going to first nights and taking part in the attendant tralala. I even dislike running into friends on ordinary nights and having to dissect or analyse what one is seeing. It always seems to end in subterfuge and betraying oneself.

But against all these idiosyncrasies of actors there are a thousand virtues, and I would like to try and point out to the layman the merits of those connected with this irresistible but heartbreaking profession. The difficulty is how to make YOU see actors as human beings. The headlines, scandals, confessions, marriages of those in the entertainment industry, which form such a feature of our daily press, have nothing to do with the creative endeavour and courage needed to produce a notable performance or production. The acute pleasure given by a performance of genius like Olivier's *Entertainer* or Guinness's in *The River Kwai* are totally unrelated to what became of Miss Diana Dors's strong-box in the Brompton Road. Yet a section of the public cannot rationalize the entertainment world, and because we are primarily there for their 'entertainment', they try to fashion us according to their whim. They cannot or do not want to believe that hard work, discipline, and above all, immense talent are essential to the artist if he is to have a lasting effect on the industry or indeed posterity.

They would rather have it that an actor's life is a bed of roses, grossly overpaid, oversexed and possibly overdrugged. They quite fail to realize that the stars who stay the course have disciplined themselves probably more completely than leaders of other professions. The path to lasting fame and success is so tricky and treacherous that many potential stars fall by the wayside, resorting to drink or at worst suicide if they cannot provide the stamina required. Time and again some talent burns itself out through too much devotion to work, and the actor with a touch of greatness must perforce face terrible loneliness and doubts as a result of the gift he knows he possesses. Nothing short of perfection will satisfy him, and he in consequence can rarely be satisfied.

When he reaches a certain pinnacle, he knows that he is being watched by millions and that public fancy can be fickle beyond belief. Not everyone wishes him well, and by becoming an international figure his privacy is invaded and it is bound to affect his private life. Fresh problems spring up, and he suddenly finds his entire existence threatened. The press sometimes help, but more often hurt, because they know the sort of things the readers want to devour. A dull star is no good to them, so any tiny foible is seized on and blown up to an immense size. Now that columnists have reached a new high in impertinent survey, it is usually safe to conclude that a bitchy or cruel interview is the result of the star's diffidence or resentment at having to put up with infringement of privacy.

It is no time before myths and legends are being spread high and wide. So-and-so is 'cold', 'has a big head', or is 'difficult'. Often I have been about to work with a performer who has a reputation of being 'difficult', only to find that the reverse was the case. Almost invariably the the 'difficult' actor or actress is highly expert, intolerant of inefficiency and stimulating to work with. It is the jumped-up 'starlet' or disappointed near-star, who is usually temperamental, rude, boring and lazy.

I have been honoured in friendship by some very distinguished members of the profession, and it is alarming to realize how my idea of them varies from the characters given them by the press, or indeed some of their fellow-actors. Yet when I try to explain to others the qualities which I find so endearing and valuable, I tend to make them sound charming but ordinary and totally different from what the listener wants to hear. It is, I fancy, because so much of their make-up (I use the word in its unnatural sense) is normal that they are able to contribute so much to the art of acting. It is only those who exist solely for display to the public and self-exhibition, who cannot adjust themselves to living like human beings. This minority do not realize the full extent of the damage until late in their lives, when they find themselves facing emptiness and loneliness.

All this sounds pompous, I suppose, and you may feel that I am the last person in the world who should make these pronunciamentos, being probably the least dedicated actor in the business. But I do know that the main reason why I have stayed so long and happily in the theatre has been because I have been lucky enough to be on the receiving end of the warmth, humanity, generosity and gaiety that actors seem to generate. They are not creatures from another world, but they do have the power to purvey the magic that still makes the theatre world a fabulous one in which to live. It is the sense of pride and the joy of living which I have personally felt, when appearing with such purveyors of magic as Gielgud or Guinness, that has been so memorable and lasting.

Such is the power of this magic that I would rather go pottering ineffectually along in the hope that every decade I may land up in another *Lady's Not for Burning*, or playing a cough and a spit in another *Horse's Mouth*. I would rather be doing this than suddenly become a great industrial tycoon with power and millions. You might say reasonably that if I was a great IT, I could then fulfil my functions as a manager, and present great actors in great plays in great theatres; but it would not be the same thing, though better for everyone else. The ultimate satisfaction for an actor is to be on a stage or screen close to 'the magic' and catch its glow and bask in its reflection. Only then can you hope to understand what any of it means, and you need to be granted one peep at this secret world and feel part of it, to be suddenly imbued with faith, a sense of security and above all to be in love with life again.

Peter Bull's Career

Books

1956: *To Sea in a Sieve*
1957: *Bulls in the Meadows*
1959: *I Know the Face, but . . .*
1961: *Not on Your Telly!*
1965: *I Say, Look Here*
1967: *It Isn't All Greek to Me*
1969: *Bear with Me*
1970: *The Teddy Bear Book*
1973: *Life is a Cucumber*
1977: *Peter Bull's Book of Teddy Bears*
1984: *A Hug of Teddy Bears*
   The Zodiac Bears

Plays

1933: (début) *If I were You; As You Desire Me; Escape Me Never*
   (London)
1935: *Escape Me Never* (NY)
1936–39: Founded and ran Perranporth Summer Theatre
1936: *The Boy David* (London)
1939: *Judgement Day* (London)
1948: *The Lady's Not for Burning* (London)
1950: *Pericles* (London); *The Lady's Not for Burning* (New York)
1951: *Figure of Fun* (London)
1952: *Under the Sycamore Tree* (London)

1953: *Second Best Bed; The Man with Expensive Tastes* (London)
1954: *The Dark is Light Enough* (London)
1955: *Waiting for Godot* (London)
1957: *The Restless Heart; Man of Distinction* (London)
1961: *Luther* (London & Paris)
1963: *Pickwick* (London); *Luther* (New York)
1965: *Pickwick* (New York)
1967: *Black Comedy* (New York)

Major Film Appearances

1937: *Sabotage*
1939: *The Ware Case*
1947: *The Turners of Prospect Road*
1948: *Oliver Twist; Saraband for Dead Lovers*
1951: *The African Queen*
1953: *The Malta Story*
1955: *Footsteps in the Fog*
1963: *Tom Jones; Dr Strangelove; The Old Dark House*
1967: *Dr Dolittle*
1969: *Lock Up Your Daughters*
1970: *The Executioner*
1972: *Up the Front; Alice's Adventures in Wonderland*
1977: *Joseph Andrews*
1978: *The Brute*
1983: *Yellowbeard*

Additionally, Peter made countless appearances in live television and radio dramas and serials as well as on chat, quiz and panel shows on both sides of the Atlantic.